LEVEL UP

—— *How to* ——
USE YOUR UNIQUE STRENGTHS
—— *to* ——
IMPROVE YOUR COMPETENCIES
—— *and* ——
REACH YOUR GOALS

MICHAEL C. OSTER

Publishing Services provided by Paper Raven Books

Printed in the United States of America

First Printing, 2020

Library of Congress Control Number: 2020907237

Paperback ISBN= 978-1-7341191-0-7
Hardback ISBN= 978-1-7341191-1-4

People love to read about work. God knows why, but they do.
—Stephen King, *On Writing*

People love to read about work. God knows why, but they do.
—Stephen King, *On Writing*

TABLE OF CONTENTS

PART II

INTRODUCTION

Life by the Inch

Here's a story about a seventh grader who lived in Southern California.

He was an average kid in every way. He got okay grades, goofed off in the hallways with his friends between classes, rode his bike everywhere, and felt awkward at dances. But there was one thing he was pretty good at—scouting. And he enjoyed it.

He had a sweet part-time job, washing and waxing his grandparents' big blue Buick on the weekends. He got to be around cars and the pay was great—the equivalent of about a hundred dollars today. His parents and grandparents lived near Pasadena, about seven miles apart. The bike ride between them was quite a solo adventure for this 11-year-old.

His grandmother, a wise soul, always took an interest in him. One day, she noticed he seemed kind of down and asked what was wrong. He told her he was really into scouting and wanted to get his Eagle Scout before entering high school. But he couldn't see how he could do it. But there was a lot to be done—too many more merit badges and projects to go.

Here's what she said to him.

"You know, Mikey, life by the inch is a cinch, by the mile is a trial."

Wow.

Life by the inch is a cinch, by the mile is a trial.

Yes, that kid was me.

I felt I had hit the wall, but my grandmother knew what I was experiencing was "the marathon in the middle"—the place where a lot of giving up occurs.

I went home and thought about what she said.

Where there had been a blurred field of merit badges and projects stretching over the horizon, a pattern started to emerge. The merit badges arranged themselves into groups of three that would require similar efforts or were related to one another. A way forward appeared. I scrambled toward it and got busy working on the badges in small batches. In the eighth grade, I was named troop leader and that summer, at age 13, I received my Eagle Scout.

I didn't know it at the time, but what I did was select two competencies I needed, Developing Plans and Executing Efficiently. I supported Developing Plans with my Arranger work strength, and I supported Executing Efficiently with my Perseverance character strength. With these two competency-strength combinations,

> Developing Plans-Arranger and
> Executing Efficiently-Perseverance,

I was able to use my strengths in specific ways and apply myself in a manner that helped me achieve a goal that was very important to me.

You've probably heard of strengths, but you may not be too familiar with competencies. Whereas our strengths are of a general nature and can be used in many ways, our competencies focus and amplify our strengths in the direction of specific goals.

As our strengths buttress our competencies, our competencies give us the ability to use our strengths in specific ways.

In this book, I'll show you how to create and use powerful competency-strength combinations to get your "merit badges" or achieve just about any goal in your life.

* * *

Success is becoming the best that you are capable of being.
—John Wooden

Are you ready to take yourself to the next level but feel a bit stuck or overwhelmed? You came to the right place. We are going to help you regain your forward momentum by using a personal and powerful methodology to become the best possible version of you. Rather than be asked to conform to a one-size-fits-all program, you will learn how to leverage your unique strengths to create potent competencies that will help you make real progress on the important issues in your life.

Confused with all the advice in self-help and leadership books?

Me too. Many seem to go too deep with unusable insights into our inner workings, or they tell us to "be like me."

Here, you will find a different approach, one that will encourage you to "be more like you."

Think of this as a practical guide to use what you've got to get where you want to go.

You will learn to use your

- *strengths* that will improve the
- *competencies* that will help you
- reach your *goals*
- in the direction of your *vision.*

Using the Level Up Method, you can be successful in *your* way. Pick something you wish to achieve, choose the competency *you* want to use to get it done, and select the strength of your choice to make it happen.

When we intentionally use our strengths to support our competencies, we are able to do things more efficiently. An added benefit: It's better for us to be defined by our competencies—specific capabilities that we use to accomplish our goals—than to be announced by our strengths—general areas in which we have potential.

If you are a high achiever, a top performer, a leader, or a high potential, you want to produce the best results you are capable of. Here we will show you step-by-step how to create and work your own personal development plan, how to form easy-to-understand and highly effective action plans, and how to reach your goals by doing what you do best.

Everything is right here—your Why, your What, and your How.

WHY	Your Vision
WHAT	Accomplishing your Goals and Objectives
HOW	Your Competency-Strength Combos

With your new approach, you can expect to produce improved results immediately. Here are three scenarios you can consign to the dustbin of history.

HAVE YOU EVER

One

Have you ever been disappointed with the results of your efforts or been told you need to improve in some way, then focused on it with remedial training and learning, only to find you could not produce the results you hoped for?

What happened?

Your approach was probably based on the model of conventional development that we have all experienced since an early age—fixing what's wrong with us. We've heard teachers tell pupils to stop doing something. But how many times have we heard a teacher encourage a student to do *more* of something? Problem is, training to minimize weaknesses isn't development, it's damage control. The common approach to weakness fixing, repetitive training without underlying talent, produces mostly disappointment and burnout.

Here you will be given permission and encouragement to discover and use more of your natural strengths in a unique way that will improve your capabilities. With the Level Up approach, not only will your journey be more pleasant, it will be a great deal more effective.

Two

Have you ever approached something in a way that has worked well for you in the past, only to see no meaningful results other than your own depleted energy?

What happened?

You may have been using your natural strengths, a good thing, to address an issue with all the effort you could muster. Strengths are very powerful but are general in their nature. To achieve something meaningful, we must be not only powerful but *specific* in our efforts. When we use *competencies* to *focus our strengths*, we can apply the right amount of energy in precisely the right direction to achieve our specific objective. The Level Up Method will show you how to create and apply potent competency-strength combinations to reach just about any objective in your life.

Three

Have you ever achieved a significant goal but, instead of feeling elated and fulfilled, you sensed an uneasy emptiness?

What happened?

Stretch goals can keep us occupied for a very long time. When completing them produces a sense of listlessness and ennui, we may have simply neglected to remind ourselves that the highest purpose of our efforts was to approach our *vision*, not just to complete some goals. With the 7 Steps to Level Up as your personal development program, you will have an easy-to-use framework that will keep your vision top of mind and refreshed as you accomplish your goals.

In *Level Up*, you will come to better understand your strengths and how to engage them effectively—by using them to support specific competencies. As you do so, you will optimize the time you spend on tasks, you will expedite your personal development and growth, and you will progress toward reaching your full potential.

With the Level Up Method™ to improve your competencies and the 7 Step framework to guide your journey, you will learn how to use your strengths to drive your life in the direction you want it to go.

- Using your strengths to improve your competencies will create *momentum.*
- Momentum gives you *confidence.*
- Behaving and working in a confident manner promotes *optimism.*
- Optimism in action is *enthusiasm.*
- Enthusiastic, confident people demonstrate *passion.*
- Passion gives you the *stamina* to stay focused on your *vision* and achieve your *goals.*

You are about to embark on a fine journey, during which you will experience small successes early as you change the trajectory of your life.

You will improve your performance, achieving better results with less wasted effort in less time.

Whenever you use a strength to improve a competency, your enthusiasm will build, and you will propel yourself one step closer to reaching your goals.

Are you ready to Level Up?

CHAPTER 1

The Level Up Method™

A New Way to Solve Problems

Life isn't about finding yourself. Life is about creating yourself.
—George Bernard Shaw

Do you feel you have what it takes to be more successful but don't quite know how to unlock your potential? Perfectly natural. Even high achievers sometimes see their progress flatten out. Often, they just took a wrong turn somewhere. Rather than keeping to the path up the mountain, they found themselves climbing a plateau. Who wants to spend a lot of time and energy only to level off? Here, you will discover how to use the Level Up Method to get you back on the path to success.

As our strengths describe *how* we can think, feel, and act, our competencies describe *what* we can do with them.

With the Level Up Method, you will see competencies bring your strengths to life in ways that will help you achieve the specific results you desire.

When Einstein said,

> *We cannot solve our problems with the same*
> *thinking we used when we created them*

he was referring to the need to be innovative in the way we address problems.

We have such a way for you, one that will help you get more out of yourself in every situation.

Here, you will learn what competencies can do, how to select the competency most likely to achieve the result you desire, and how to engage your signature strengths in support of that competency to meet the challenge you face.

As your strengths supply propulsion, your competencies will provide direction.

Conjoined, your competencies and strengths form powerful competency-strength combinations. Applying just the right strength to support a competency, and using them together, is the Level Up Method. This method is *your* innovative way to respond to opportunities, deliver superior performance, and solve the problems in your life in a way that ensures they stay solved.

A valuable feature of the Method is its ease of use. Every scenario for applying it has only three moving parts—the objective you are working on, the competency you will use to accomplish it, and the strength that will best assist the competency to produce the results you want.

Accomplish an	by engaging a	that is supported by a
Objective	←Competency	←Strength

The more you focus on these three ingredients, the greater will be your progress toward your goals, and the more quickly you will begin to narrow the distance between your intention and your impact. The shorter the distances between your objective, the competency, and your strength, the better.

How to do that?

When you create a competency-strength combination, you directly link the competency to the strength most likely to support it. Like this:

Objective←Competency-Strength Combination

When you form and use a combination a few times, the competency and the strength weave themselves together into one. The strength becomes part of your competency and your competency improves the potency of your strength. These competency-strength combos can propel you toward your objectives quickly and powerfully.

You've heard of weapons of destruction?

Think of competency-strength combos as your weapons of *con*struction. Use them to make progress on any issue in your life.

Have you ever experienced the stress from feeling that your life is in charge of you instead of the other way around? Who hasn't!

An additional benefit of incorporating the Level Up Method into your everyday thinking will be the reduction in stress and the increase in self-confidence you will experience as you begin to take charge of your life, one competency-strength combo at a time.

In the pages ahead, I will give you many examples of how to use the character strengths identified by the VIA Institute and the work strengths identified by Gallup. I will also provide a few concepts and scenarios to help you form your own ideas about how to use your strengths so you're making progress on the important issues in your life.

VIA's and Gallup's extensive investigations into character strengths and work strengths are based on many years of solid research. My insights into how we can use our strengths are based on my years in organizations and my observations of how high achievers and high potentials can use these findings. My richest experiences have come from being a shirtsleeve leader, working in the trenches with others to solve problems and get things done. A few lofty job titles aside, I have made my best contributions when serving in the role of player-coach.

I only wish I had known sooner about my strengths. I would have been more effective and could have helped myself and others avoid a lot of the missteps we made. Coulda, shoulda.

FILL THE GAP

When assembling your competency-strength combos to achieve your objectives, also keep your larger aspiration in mind—

reaching the goals that will help you move in the direction of your vision. A Gap Analysis can help you picture the area between where you are and where you want to go.

A Gap Analysis is a visual comparison of your actual performance with your potential or desired performance.

Top line   Where you want to go: your vision, your potential

Bottom line   Where you will go if you don't change anything

Between the lines is the space to fill—the difference between the present you and the desired future you. Use the Gap to visualize the actual and possible trajectories of your life.

Just seeing the void between the lines will give you motivation to take yourself from who you are to who you can become.

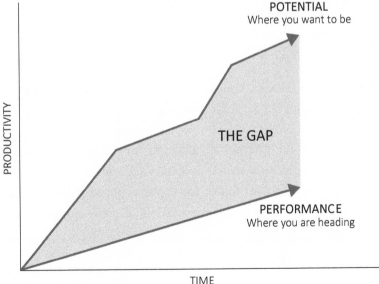

Each of us has a Gap between the vision for ourselves and the reality of where we are. Between the two lie the opportunities for our personal growth.

The Level Up Method and your powerful competency-strength combos will help you make incremental and intentional improvements to fill the Gap.

What if your progress doesn't resemble the top line in the graph? No one's does. A more accurate portrayal of our lives is this little funny from Demetri Martin:

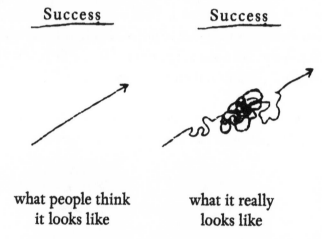

Just keep your focus on your vision and be fine with your squiggle. If you stick with it, it will all work out.

Over time, as you intentionally engage your strengths to improve the competencies best suited to achieving your objectives, you will find yourself more often at the top of your game. Your ability to repeatedly produce positive results will improve and your Gap will shrink.

An additional benefit to organizations is that using the Level Up Method will increase the number of high performers and great leaders in your company.

As Oprah says,

> *How you spend your time defines who you are.*

Now, let's crack open the strengths library and discover how to use the unique and mighty abilities we each have.

PART I

Your Strengths

You Are Unique

Hide not your talents. They for use were made. What is a sundial in the shade?
—Benjamin Franklin

I magine you have inherited a store—a nice store.

Stocked on the shelves of your store are your strengths. Some, the better ones, are on the upper shelves, on the level between your head and chest. Most of your strengths are on the shelves in the middle. Many useful items are here. The few on the lower shelves mainly sit there, gathering dust.

Other people also have stores, but nobody has a store exactly like yours.

You may use the items in your store however you wish—for yourself, to share with others, or to offer for sale. But, unlike the items in a real store, when you take your strengths off the shelf and use them, they not only remain on the shelf but get bigger and better every time, like some *Alice in Wonderland* paradox.

In this chapter, you will see how to discover and utilize the strengths that define your character—your mental and moral qualities—and the strengths you can draw upon to accomplish things, alone or with others in a work environment.

FIRST, IDENTIFY YOUR STRENGTHS

Strengths are tasks or actions you can do well. These include knowledge, proficiencies, skills, and talents. People use their traits and abilities to complete work, relate with others, and achieve goals.[1]

How do you know what your own strengths are, and whether they're shoulder high, waist high, or at ankle level on your figurative store shelves?

Well, you can take an assessment, and we'll talk about the two best assessments out there shortly. Or, with some reflection and intuition, you may be able to identify your own strengths.

Think of times when you felt happily productive. What were you doing? Were you alone, with others, at work, at play?

That pleasant sense of usefulness you experienced was from engaging your signature strengths, the ones that are most robust in you. Intentionally or not, you gathered a few from the shelves for use in your life.

---

1 YourDictionary, s.v. "Examples of Strengths," accessed March 2020, https://examples.yourdictionary.com/examples-of-strengths.html.

THREE WAYS TO DETERMINE WHAT YOUR STRENGTHS ARE

1   Take a *qualitative* approach and create your own strengths inventory. An interesting DIY project.

Start with a clean sheet or, if you like, consider the strengths investigated by others. Some likely candidates can be found in:

- *Character Strengths and Virtues*, Christopher Peterson and Martin Seligman
- Signature Strength Questionnaire (SSQ-72), University of Toronto
- Personal Strengths Inventory, Truity
- The DiSC Profile, Wiley

Make a list of the ones that best describe your unique characteristics.

Because it can be hard to be knowledgeable and truthful about ourselves, we have the next method as an alternative.

2   Take a *quantitative* approach and take an online assessment or two. See what a trusted survey says about you.

To learn what our signature character strengths are and how we can each be a better person, my favorite assessment is the free VIA Character Strengths Survey. Plan to spend about 25 minutes taking this. You can find it at www.viacharacter.org.

To learn what our signature performance strengths are and how we can be more effective working with others, my favorite assessment is CliftonStrengths®[2] from Gallup. It will take you about 40 minutes. You can find it at www.gallup.com.

Almost 50 million people have taken the VIA and Gallup strengths surveys. Ninety percent of Fortune 500 companies use them.

3 *Mix and match*. Trust, but verify.

Whether you create your own list of strengths or adopt those in a report from a survey, give your intuition an opportunity to consider both approaches. Then confirm or revise what you feel are the strengths that most accurately describe your true abilities.

I have been in problem-solving and leadership roles at both for-profit and nonprofit organizations. Now, as a coach and advisor to those who want to level up, I have discovered that each of us can do so with the straightforward process of using our signature strengths to support and improve the competencies we need to accomplish our goals.

This part of the book provides my observations of how our character and work strengths show up most often in our everyday lives. With your reports on the 24 VIA character strengths and the 34 Gallup themes of talent related to performance, you will be provided with their definitions and recommendations for how to use them.

---

2 formerly called StrengthsFinder

The interpretations presented here are based upon the words VIA and Gallup chose as the names for their strengths. We assume they adopted common terms that most accurately capture the essence of the strengths for which they survey. So we focus our interpretations on the standard definitions and common usages of those terms. To avoid confusing the names of the strengths with their common usage, these words will appear here in two ways: in lowercase for everyday usage, and capitalized when we are using them to refer to a VIA character strength or Gallup work strength. Tempting as it may be, we do not compare, contrast, or attempt to reconcile VIA's character strengths with Gallup's work strengths. To quote Shakespeare, "That way madness lies."[3]

The purpose of this section is to provide you a general understanding of strengths, to set the stage for how you will use them to improve your competencies with the Level Up Method™.

If you are artistically inclined, consider your strengths as you would the keys on a piano.[4]

If 24 character strengths and 34 work strengths sounds like a lot to deal with, think of how you can draw upon these 58 strengths as pianists use the 88 keys on a piano; they do not attempt to use every possible note, but play select combinations that produce all kinds of wonderful results.

---

3 William Shakespeare, *King Lear,* 3.4.21. References are to act, scene, and line.
4 Another analogy of strengths to piano keys can be found in Marcus Buckingham and Donald O. Clifton, *Now, Discover Your Strengths,* (Washington, DC: Gallup Press, 2001), 12.

The pianist doesn't play all 88 keys. She plays in the range where she can use her abilities and feelings in a way that most pleases the audience and herself. Think of yourself as a musician who can produce beautiful and original music within a range. Learning your talents will help you identify the notes that are the best ones for you to use when making *your* music. You get to decide what kind of music you wish to make. Adventurous? Contemplative? Romantic? It can be any of these or something else. Your choice. When you play the pieces you want to play, your practice will be more effective and enjoyable because you will use your strengths in the best way—with intention.

But, you say, I don't have 88 strengths from which to choose.

Worry not. Thanks to Steinway, the piano with 88 keys is a relatively modern improvement, if you consider the 1880s to be modern. Mozart's piano in the late 1700s had but 40 keys. A bit later, in the early 1800s, Beethoven's had 48 keys. With about 50 percent of the notes that would be available to them now, they were able to produce masterpieces that endure to this day. (If you have the dough, about $300,000, you can now buy a piano with 201 keys.)

Playing your music your way, you will engage the strengths that are the most useful, natural, and pleasurable to use. Irving Berlin never learned to play the piano. And when he did play, he could only play in F-sharp. With only 36 black keys to choose from, look what he did with what *he* had![5]

---

5 Irving Berlin (1888–1989) was an Israeli-born American composer and lyricist. During his 60-year career, he wrote an estimated 1,500 songs, including scores for Broadway shows and Hollywood films. Berlin is widely considered one of the greatest songwriters in American history, despite his extremely limited piano skills.

For those who are more scientifically minded, you might consider the 58 strengths as you would the periodic table of 118 elements. It all started in 1809 with the identification of the first 47 elements. Eventually, with the discovery of plutonium in 1940, the number of naturally occurring elements climbed to 94. The elements added more recently, 95 to 118, do not occur naturally but can be synthesized in laboratory experiments or nuclear reactors. The last three were discovered in 2016.

And what can be produced using these 118 ingredients? *Everything!*

Here is the BIG IDEA of Part I:

The desirable aspects of your character and the unique ways you solve problems and work with others are your strengths. Your most potent ones are called your signature strengths.

Your
CHARACTER TRAITS

+

your
ABILITY TO COMPLETE WORK

=

your
STRENGTHS

Whether you use the 58 character and work strengths from VIA and Gallup or the ones on a list of your own making, here's a simple process to detect which ones will be most useful to you.

NEXT, SORT YOUR STRENGTHS

A good first exercise is to divide your character strengths and your work strengths into three tiers.

Top Tier
Your Signature Strengths—these are "always on" for you

Starting with the top strengths in one of your reports or from your own list built from your experiences and intuition, draw a line under the group of strengths that you use most frequently and effectively. If these are the ones that reside in your top quartile, you may find you have 6 signature character strengths and 9 signature work strengths

Bottom Tier
Your Lesser Strengths—unlikely to be of much use to you

Starting at the bottom, draw a line *over* the group of strengths you rarely use. These are your lesser strengths. If these are the ones that dwell in your bottom quartile, you may have 6 lesser character strengths and 9 lesser work strengths. They are infrequently of much use to you, and we are not going to make any attempt to elevate them. Just acknowledge their position and move on. Some strengths must be at the bottom. These are yours.

Middle Tier
Your Intermediate Strengths—the big group in the middle

Use these to lend a hand to your signature strengths and help you accomplish a goal or objective.

NOW, USE YOUR STRENGTHS...

The Level Up Method will help you intentionally engage your strengths to improve your competencies as you become the best possible version of you. But how to know which strengths to use for what?

When you receive the report from the VIA or Gallup strengths survey, you will notice the makers of the assessment assign your strengths to categories they have created to help you better understand what to use their strengths for. VIA's categories focus on virtue; Gallup's focus on leadership.

...WHERE THEY CAN BE OF THE MOST BENEFIT TO YOU

We have for you here a structure, the 5 Sets of Strengths, to which you can assign both types of strengths in the groups where they gather to help us think or act. In each of the next chapters, we will explore one of the 5 Sets of Strengths.

The 5 Sets of Strengths

THINKING THOROUGHLY
INTERACTING WITH OTHERS
HAVING A POSITIVE EFFECT ON OTHERS
PERFORMING WITH EXCELLENCE
ALIGNING TO YOUR VALUES

We will see how your character and work strengths can be useful to you in each set as you solve problems, work with others, get stuff done, and stay true to your values.

Rather than a rigid prescriptive system, consider this as a flexible set of suggested homes for your strengths. As you begin to understand and apply your strengths, you may find that some of your strengths will serve you better in sets other than the ones we use in our illustrations. And some strengths will also be able to help you think and do things in other sets. Consider these as your "free-range" strengths. They don't have to permanently reside in just one set. If some of your signature strengths can serve you better in a different set, feel free to reassign them to different sets. For reference, in Appendix A: The 5 Sets of Strengths you will see the five general sets and the character and work strengths you might consider using to demonstrate each.

THE W WORD
WHAT ABOUT WEAKNESSES?

Success is achieved by developing our strengths, not by eliminating our weaknesses.
—Marilyn vos Savant, columnist of "Ask Marilyn"
and holder of highest recorded IQ

A weakness is anything that gets in the way of your success. If you engage it, it will drain your energy and block you from being productive. Weaknesses can't be fixed, they can only be managed. Get a little better at them, work around them, or ignore them.

Your lesser strengths may be among them. If you can, just avoid using them.

Remember, it's only a weakness if it gets in your way. If it doesn't cause you to step on a rake, let it go. Here's Coach John Wooden on the subject: "Do not let what you cannot do interfere with what you can do."

Most of us enjoy doing things we're good at. The things we don't enjoy doing? We're probably not very good at them. From a strengths perspective, we should be spending our time and energies elsewhere. Yet we are often directed to fix what's wrong with us. "Opportunities for improvement," they're called.

Those things you don't do well? You now have permission to stop doing them!

Have you ever heard a parent tell a child that he can be anything he wants to be?

Here's the catch—actually, we *can't* be anything we want to be.

The idea that everyone can be anything they want to be if they work hard to fix their weaknesses leads to a lot of frustration and wasted effort that could have been better used in the service of strengths.

Training to minimize weaknesses isn't development, it's damage control.

Improvement requires persistence, but the danger of repetitive training that does not engage a natural strength is burnout.

> *Focusing on weaknesses leads to frustration.*
> *Focusing on strengths leads to success.*

For many of us, the tendency during our entire lives has been to focus on our weaknesses—at school, at work, and in our relationships. For a perspective on how this came to be, see the "Fixing Weaknesses Goes Way Back" essay at the end of the chapter.

In school, test scores reflected what we did *not* know. Except for essay tests, they provided no insights into areas where we excelled. Contrast this conventional development approach with strengths-based development.

Conventional Development	*Strengths-Based Development*
Identify areas of weakness	Identify areas of strength
Train to reduce weaknesses	Train to practice and develop strengths

Happily, we are seeing an increase of strengths-based development movements in both education and organizations.

But there is one weakness of which we do have to be wary.

> *Our greatest weakness lies in giving up. The most certain way to succeed is always to try just one more time.*
> —Thomas Edison

Thomas Edison and Henry Ford were friends. In 1929, Henry Ford built Greenfield Village in Dearborn, a suburb of Detroit. For Greenfield, Ford acquired many of Edison's artifacts and one of his power plants. He used them to recreate Edison's Menlo Park Complex. It was in this New Jersey laboratory that Edison perfected the lightbulb in 1880. If you haven't been to Greenfield, consider it for your bucket list. For his demonstration village, Ford assembled an immense collection of buildings and inventions from the Who's Who of the 19th century.

Fun fact: Edison and Ford were members of a traveling mastermind group, The Vagabonds. Other members were President Warren G. Harding, Harvey Firestone, and Luther Burbank. Imagine if you were invited to attend one of their meetings.

Strolling through Edison's laboratory produces hushed wonderment among the visitors. Even children, sensing that something important happened here, become calm. It's a very simple and humble place. But what strikes you is that this is a place where real work, the unglamorous kind, was done.

Try, try, then try again. Until the needle moves or something happens. With ordinary materials and incredible persistence, Edison was trying to produce the uncommon. Eventually, he perfected the lightbulb and the world changed.

Outside the building is this sign:

> *I never did anything by accident, nor did any*
> *of my inventions come by accident.*
> *They came by work.*
> —Thomas Edison, inventor

What strengths do you think Edison possessed? His character strengths of Curiosity, Creativity, and Perseverance must have been off the charts. Likewise for his work strengths, Analytical and Achiever.

We can't all be Edisons. Only Edison could be Edison. But we all can do the work and try just one more time.

As American author Steven Pressfield says,

Our job in this lifetime is not to shape ourselves into some ideal we imagine we ought to be, but to find out who we already are and become it.[6]

FEELING YACHTY?

As we go through these strength sets together in the upcoming chapters, remember that you can use your strengths

- as an ANCHOR when you need to hold your position,
- as a RUDDER when you need to change direction,
- as an ENGINE to provide forward momentum from within, and
- as a SAIL to leverage your environment and propel you forward.

In Part II: The Competencies, we reveal 17 productive ways you can apply your strengths to reach your goals. Your competencies will provide the conduits through which you can use your strengths to make real progress—as you harness your potential and become the next better version of you.

FIXING WEAKNESSES GOES WAY BACK: A PERSPECTIVE

Since their introduction, codes of conduct and laws have been steadying influences on our base inclinations, our weaknesses if

6 Steven Pressfield, *The War of Art* (Black Irish Books, 2002).

you will. When people interact, they need guidelines to maintain order.

It all began 50 centuries ago, in the richest and most densely populated place in the world—Mesopotamia, the area between the Tigris and Euphrates. Some time around the 32nd century BC, the Sumerians invented writing. A thousand years later, in the 22nd century BC, they created the first laws. Just to the north, around the 18th century BC, King Hammurabi developed Babylonian law. If you broke these laws, no "three hots and a cot" in some cushy prison for you. You paid the price immediately. An eye for an eye.

1,500 miles to the southwest of Mesopotamia is Mt. Sinai, where Moses received the 10 Commandments. They are thought to have been written somewhere between the 16th and 13th centuries BC. The 10 Commandments were not exactly laws, but neither were they the 10 Suggestions. At least they, unlike laws, encouraged you to do *more* of some things, two to be exact.

Fast forward to modern times and you in your formative years.

Unless you were a naturally good little boy or girl (I wasn't), did it sometimes seem that everyone was on your case at one time or another? Parental control, school rules, church rules, laws that told you not to ride your bike on the sidewalk, and whether to WALK or DON'T WALK. Don't get me wrong—I *needed* to be told all that stuff.

The two sets of rules I was fine with growing up were the ones associated with activities that also offered opportunities to use my strengths—to do whatever I wanted so long as I didn't break the rules. In sports and games, the price of admission is playing by the rules. From capture the flag to football, from Go Fish to chess. If you play by the rules, you can pretty much do whatever else you want—be creative and burn off some energy. When you finally get your driver's license and have your first real taste of freedom, you get a whole new set of thou-shalt-nots to deal with. Starting with speed limits.

This what-not-to-do approach to life is baked into us at an early age. It probably has to be that way until we become responsible adults. (Have you noticed that girls reach this point earlier than boys? Okay, men.) Our early years are spent in human development—growing physically, cognitively, and psychosocially. At adulthood, we can transition from human development to personal development, the subject of our book.

But the Mesopotamians didn't have the chance for much personal development. If average lifespans were 20 to 35 years, they spent most of their years growing up and needing rules to keep them from leading with their weaknesses.

With our longer lifespans, we are more fortunate. Once we tip from human development to personal development, we can concentrate less on our weaknesses and more on our strengths. This is where the real pleasure of adulthood begins.

CHAPTER 2

Thinking Thoroughly

Increase Wisdom and Make Plans

with your Character Strengths[7]

CREATIVITY®   JUDGEMENT®   PERSPECTIVE®

CURIOSITY®   LOVE OF LEARNING®

with your Work Strengths[8]

ANALYTICAL®   IDEATION®   LEARNER®

CONTEXT®   INPUT®   STRATEGIC®

FUTURISTIC®   INTELLECTION®

We begin our exploration of strengths with those that reside in our Thinking Thoroughly set. We'll address each of these thirteen strengths with a look at:

- the signals it sends
- what it feels like
- how to use it
- engaging with others who have it

---

7 from the VIA Institute
8 from Gallup, Inc.

Each of our strengths within the Thinking Thoroughly set can be useful when creating a vision, processing information, making decisions, and putting in place the plans that will enable you to accomplish your goals.

THINKING THOROUGHLY WITH YOUR CHARACTER STRENGTHS

Creativity®
The ones who ask, "I wonder what would happen if…?" are likely blessed with the strength of Creativity. They are always looking for new ways to do things.

If this sounds like you, you love bringing new concepts and strategies into your life and to others as you work on projects with them. Your Creativity broadens your outlook on the ways available to solve problems.

Use your Creativity to bring new perspectives to artistic expression and to help others see new ways to consider issues they are facing.

If you are grappling with a sticky situation in your personal life or at work, engage someone with Creativity to help you brainstorm what your options are. He may help you find windows and doors you were not aware existed and explore how you might move through them to reach an acceptable resolution to your issue.

Curiosity®
When Columbus set sail, he was under no delusion the earth was flat. That idea was resolved by Pythagoras in 500 BC. But Columbus, and his sponsor Queen Isabella, did have a great deal of *curiosity* about the potential for a lucrative western trade

route to China. If he knew that the sparsely populated North American continent would be in his way, we would probably not be marching in Columbus Day parades today.

With Curiosity, you have a natural interest in pursuing new information and experiences to deepen your understanding of a variety of subjects.

Use your Curiosity to explore, investigate, and learn new things about any topic of interest to you. Think of your strength of Curiosity as your "license to learn."

If you are pondering the way forward on an issue and your path doesn't feel like the right one, ask someone with strong Curiosity to help you evaluate your options. The first thing she may do is ask why you are going about it the way you are. This simple question may help you see how your approach may or may not be the best one. The next question she may ask is, "What else have you considered?" When your choices seem limited, one with strong Curiosity can help you find new options to pursue.

Judgement®
(abbr. for Judgement/Critical Thinking®)
When you and another with whom you are solving a problem asks, "Have we considered...?" you may have been given a clue that you are in the presence of one with solid Judgement.

If Judgement is one of your signature strengths, you carefully examine all the facts and issues that will help you make an objective decision. You consider each bit of relevant information from multiple points of view before concluding your analysis.

Your ability to think critically, to weigh all the evidence, is rooted firmly in our set of Thinking Thoroughly strengths. With few preconceived ideas about how to best address a new issue, you carefully consider all the facts before making your choice of the best way to proceed.

If you find yourself under pressure to make a decision in an emotionally charged environment, ask one with strong Judgement to help you sort through the noise before you choose a course of action. His open-mindedness and ability to consider all the options, not just the ones he may personally favor, will add clarity and objectivity to your evaluation process.

Love of Learning®
Someone who enjoys visiting museums and taking classes where they can learn new things loves the acquisition of new information and experiences.

While others may be bored by the absence of activity associated with acquiring new information, you are excited about the mental and emotional stimulation these bring you.

Some associate going to the library with their early experiences of mandatory study hall or detention. For you, the library is heaven. You relish everything about it: the smell, the challenge of navigating the stacks, and all that knowledge in the books and media.

At home or at work, pulling at the thread of a new concept on the internet can bring the whole tapestry onto your screen. Next thing you know, it's two hours later.

Your natural tendency toward comprehension will speed up your ability to develop and explore all kinds of things. Use it to increase your own body of knowledge and to be an interesting conversation partner with others in talks about things of interest to both of you.

If you are trying to solve a problem and cannot see how to achieve the desired result with one of your options, ask someone with Love of Learning among her signature strengths to help you further explore the most promising choices you have. She may happily join the effort with her own in-depth investigation to discover new aspects about one or more of your alternatives.

Perspective®

Do you know someone who is a "big picture person," one to whom the world makes more sense than to the rest of us? He is likely one who has the gift of a broad point of view.

If this sounds like you, when you listen to a presentation or a conversation your mind takes into consideration many other things that help frame the discussion topic—your experiences and lessons learned from your previous encounters with it, how it compares with similar and tangential concepts, and where it can be of service to something you want to accomplish.

Use your Perspective to take a broader view. We *choose* to see mostly what's directly in front of us. But, if we extend our arms away from our body, most of us *can* see our fingertips when they are 180° apart. That's peripheral vision, and it shows us how broad our field of vision can be. When you are charging full speed ahead, look out the window to your left and right every once in a while to gain a sense of what's around you, not just where you are *headed.*

When you wish to achieve something but your choices seem limited, engage one with Perspective to help you identify additional options. While you are inside your situation, he will be able to see it from the outside and can help you see the bigger picture.

THINKING THOROUGHLY WITH YOUR WORK STRENGTHS

Analytical®

Analytical people tend to take a practical point of view rather than an emotional one. Think of those who ask all the questions. Every time they do so, or an answer is given to their questions, the rest of us learn a little more about the topic. Always on the side of truth, Analytical people are objective problem solvers and make decisions based upon the evidence.

If this sounds like you, you bring logic to the decision-making process. Your ability to apply rigorous attention to an issue often reveals patterns and connections between its different aspects. You use your natural investigative ability to sort through information, organize it, and make it more understandable for others.

When deeper understanding of an issue is required, your ability to perform thorough analysis enables you to be an objective problem solver.

If you have a project that requires deep fact finding, partner with someone who is naturally Analytical. She will ask the tough questions and help you think in ways that will better inform your decisions.

Context®

Gallup tells us those with the strength Context can see and compare the past and the present. They can see the chain of events that got us to where we are today.

If you can think contextually, you value experience and the lessons learned from the past. You can see the linear nature of past-present-future progressions and can use what has happened in the past to open up opportunities in the present and plans for the future.

When you think with your Context, you can pull from the experiences of others and yourself to solve problems as they arise. In so doing, you help ensure that mistakes made in the past are not repeated.

When more fully understanding the past will help you make better sense of the present, partner with someone who can think contextually about the situation at hand and the circumstances informing it. When he does, it may give you a sense of continuity that will be helpful as you chart a course forward.

Futuristic®

Those who are drawn to thinking about what the future might hold are energized by what can *be* more than by what *is*.

If you naturally enjoy thinking about what is to come, you are inspired by what it might bring. You anticipate what might happen in the future and can imagine it in vivid detail. You can see it so clearly that, sometimes, the present feels like the past.

Most strengths can be used to *push* you in a direction you want to go. With your forward thinking, you feel *pulled* toward your vision of what is possible.

To consider what is possible in your life, engage one with Futuristic to help you think about the possible outcomes of your plans. He will bring you a sense of hope and energy around the future. And his vivid descriptions of it may inspire you to act with conviction.

Ideation®

Those who ask, "What if...?" consider issues from multiple perspectives and can generate new ideas around any topic. As they form ideas and concepts, they often put a new spin on things, broadening the ways in which a subject is considered and evaluated.

If this sounds like you, you can generate new ideas of your own on a variety of subjects. When you do, you enjoy considering the new perspectives you bring to existing concepts. You have the ability to connect existing ideas to solve a problem or create ideas not previously considered.

Use your Ideation to bring new thinking and new views to the table for further consideration. Your constant pursuit of creation enables you to see things from multiple points of view.

When you are stuck, ask others who often demonstrate new ways of thinking for a few ideas. They can be excellent brainstorming partners. Their fresh ideas will expand your perspective and may help you build bridges between the thoughts of others.

Input®

The ones who say, "Tell me more..." love gathering new information, sorting and storing it.

If this sounds like you, you enjoy collecting facts, objects, and experiences. You always want to know more. By nature, you are curious and inquisitive. You enjoy performing research and absorbing information that may be useful later. You love to acquire knowledge about a wide variety of topics.

Seek new assignments where you can use your inquisitive nature to deepen your understanding of a subject, expanding and adding to what you already know about it. Make yourself accessible to others who may be served by information you have on a subject interesting or useful to them.

When you need some fresh ideas on an issue, talk with someone who enjoys broadening and deepening his knowledge. He may know something about your topic or can show you how to seek and process new information.

Intellection®

Those who say, "Let me think about it and get back to you" naturally enjoy the process of understanding things more deeply. They are conscientious and often bring perspective and insights that others may have missed.

If Intellection is one of your strengths, you like to think. When lost in your thoughts, you feel bliss. Quiet reflection is a favorite activity, considering what transpired in the past and what is to come.

When and where you use your strength of understanding is also important, since you probably have times, places, or activities where you make your best discoveries. When you replicate these situations, you promote thinking in ways that are pleasurable and useful. You enjoy thinking about topics you know something about, then furthering your understanding of those subjects. You take your time to consider a project before initiating action.

When something you are working on will benefit from further investigation, join with someone who is good with concepts and likes to think in depth. He may not have the answers, but his questions will further your understanding of the issue.

Learner®
The ones who say, "Let me look into that" love the process of discovery. They will put in the time and effort to investigate a new concept.

If this sounds like you, you are inquisitive and love to learn. Self-improvement is important and you enjoy exploring new topics. You are confident taking on new challenges and helping others discover more about a subject. You are delighted to be on journeys that take you from not knowing to knowing.

Give yourself opportunities to learn and broaden your knowledge base. Use your capacity for discovery to contribute knowledge to areas in which you are interested. Sharing your knowledge with others will be enjoyable and add value to their endeavors.

When you need to find new ways to reach a goal, someone who naturally enjoys learning new things may bring new and relevant approaches to addressing your issues and solving problems. Her natural curiosity will help you explore the alternatives, informing your choice of the best path to success.

Strategic®

When making plans, those who ask, "Have we considered...?" see the big picture. They are creative, conceptual, can spot the underlying themes of an issue, and organize them to achieve the best outcome.

If this sounds like you, you can naturally spot patterns, identify the alternatives, and form the plans that make the most sense.

Trust your insights and put your ideas to work. When you use your broad perspective to consider challenges and opportunities, approach them as you would when playing a board game. Thinking several moves ahead, you can make the moves that will best set you up for a win. Seeing the desired result helps you find the best path to get from where you are to where you want to go.

When you feel lost in the details of a project you are working on, ask someone who can think strategically for his opinion. He may help you see what your most important and achievable goals are and how to allocate your resources to address them. From a bit loftier viewpoint, you might gain some clarity on which next steps will result in the progress you desire.

CHAPTER 3

Interacting with Others

Connect with People and Support Them

with your Character Strengths[9]

FAIRNESS®   LOVE®   TEAMWORK®

HONESTY®   SOCIAL INTELLIGENCE®

with your Work Strengths[10]

EMPATHY®   INCLUDER®   POSITIVITY®

HARMONY®   INDIVIDUALIZATION®   RELATOR®

When we understand the needs and feelings of people, we can connect more deeply with them. People who appreciate others and form bonds with them interact with an intensity that helps them form powerful collaborative relationships. They can build the strong personal alliances that bind people together.

We'll address each of these 11 Interacting with Others strengths with a look at:

---

9 from the VIA Institute
10 from Gallup, Inc.

- the signals it sends
- what it feels like
- how to use it
- engaging with others who have it

Each of these can be valuable when you are connecting with, working with, and leading people.

INTERACTING WITH OTHERS WITH YOUR CHARACTER STRENGTHS

Fairness®

Say, what's that quality we want our deities and judges to have? You know the one, where they treat everyone the same and uniformly interpret how the laws apply to defendants or parties in a dispute? Fairness.

When you treat people fairly, you bring an absence of personal bias and an abundance of inclusiveness to all your interactions. You are equitable and impartial to one and all.

With the low signal-to-noise level of our daily lives, this strength can take conscious effort to maintain amid all the distractions that are constantly coming our way. A fine example of how we can help ourselves be fairer is a device used in the audition process for musicians who wish to join an orchestra. As the small selection committee sits near the center of the hall, the aspiring musician performs behind a screen. Short, tall, male, female, skinny, fat... none of that matters. All that counts is how they play.

If we want to bring more fairness into our dealings with others, we can ask someone with a signature strength of Fairness to help us remove details and opinions that are irrelevant to our being just. He can help us identify the most essential and valid information to consider when making decisions that affect others.

Honesty®

If you know someone who can be counted upon to speak the truth, you are probably acquainted with one whose beliefs and behaviors demonstrate he feels that "honesty is the best policy."[11]

If this sounds like you, you are sincere and straightforward with yourself and others.

If Honesty is one of your signature strengths, you make a trustworthy companion on any journey.

Use your Honesty to consistently demonstrate your integrity to others. In return, they will give you their confidence. When you exhibit your Honesty, you are perceived as reliable and dependable.

If you are at an upper level in an organization and want to know more about what is really going on in the field, here is a tip. Ask one who is out there and has Honesty as a signature strength to help you learn more about how things are for "the boots on the ground." If you're lucky, and this person also has the strength of bravery, he may be able to speak truth to power.

---

11 Sir Edwin Sandys, in the English settlement of Jamestown, Virginia, said it first in 1599. Two hundred years later, in 1799, Benjamin Franklin used it in a letter to Edward Bridgen.

Love®

Do you know someone who places a high value on their close relationships with others? Chances are you are acquainted with a person whose signature strengths include Love. Not ones to play it close to the vest, those who feel and exhibit Love openly share with others their true feelings.

If this sounds like you, you have the need and ability to connect with others in ways where all can demonstrate their care for one another. You radiate warmth and appreciate it when others do the same.

Use your strength of Love to bring you closer to those who matter most. When you do so, they may respond in a similar manner. Using the strength of Love is a powerful way to create and maintain strong give-and-take relationships.

When you are feeling drained by the busyness of your life, carve out some quality time to spend with one of your close friends who counts Love among their signature strengths. A peaceful interlude within the security of a strong relationship can provide a welcome respite from what is frantic in your world.

Social Intelligence®

If you know someone who can read a room and always knows the right thing to say, you are probably acquainted with someone with high Social Intelligence. She can simultaneously understand her feelings and thoughts and those of others around her.

If this sounds like you, you understand and appreciate what is different about others. This enables you to deal with a variety of people and maintain social relationships with them. You are comfortable with social change and can exhibit tact when speaking with others.

When you demonstrate your Social Intelligence, your presence gives others a level of comfort. This strength can be a useful one to bring to your collaborative relationships. Others, feeling understood by you, will be more willing to give their best to the task at hand.

When you find yourself stalled in a negotiation, enlist someone with strong Social Intelligence to help you understand the other side's position. She may help you gain valuable insights into the motives and feelings of the other party. Equipped with this new intelligence, you may be able to more easily reach an outcome that is beneficial to both parties by giving the other side some of what they want and need.

Teamwork®

If you are fortunate enough to know someone who "plays well with others," you know a team player—one who enjoys working with others to achieve a common goal. Teamwork, the work of teams, is the strength that helps us collaborate with others to achieve a common goal.

If this sounds like you, you are loyal to your team and committed to doing what you can to help it be successful. When you are with your team, you put the priorities of the team above your own. Then you get busy and do your part to help the team reach its goal.

Engaging your Teamwork strength will help you as you help others. Doing so, you will feel more engaged in your activities and will earn the trust of your comrades. Teamwork isn't just for sports or business. It is for any activity where you join with another. You and your significant other are a team, one that probably has a lot of goals for just two people. You and a friend working at the table on a puzzle are a team. And you and your volunteer sous chef preparing a meal for your guests are a team.

When, on a project, you find that you have bitten off more than you can chew, ask someone with the Teamwork strength for their opinion. He may help you take a step back and see that a better way forward will include sharing the work with others. It could be a win-win-win. You get out of overwhelm and enjoy the benefits of human interaction, others feel more engaged, and all reap the rewards when many hands lighten the load.

INTERACTING WITH OTHERS WITH YOUR WORK STRENGTHS

Empathy®

The person who says, "I feel your pain" is one who senses the emotions of others and can speak up for those whose voices are not being heard.

If this sounds like you, you are intuitive and can understand the feelings of others. Your ability to do so enables you to form relationships of great emotional depth.

When you use this emotional intelligence to communicate with and lead others, you do so with an understanding of their feelings and points of view. This provides them comfort and a sense that you are with them on their journey. You know your ability to feel what others feel is not the same as embracing those feelings and points of view for yourself.

When you want to know how your messages are being received by others, ask someone who can identify with what others are feeling to share her observations about how you can be more relevant to others. Also seek her opinion before you make a significant decision. She can serve as your emotional barometer, helping you understand the impact it will have on others.

Harmony®

Those who, in a heated discussion, say "Okay, let's take it down a notch" believe in the value of togetherness. They help us see that what we have in common is more powerful than our differences.

If this sounds like you, you are more interested in what unites us than what divides us. You find conflict to be unproductive and look for areas of agreement. As you steer around disagreements, you encourage people to work together.

Detecting where agreement can be reached, you can help others move from conflict to resolution. As you encourage people to work together, you help them find opportunities for collaboration.

When you have a group of people with differing opinions on an issue that needs concurrence, ask someone who is adept at avoiding discord to be one of your advisors. He can help those with opposing viewpoints find common ground and work together. When emotions are running high, he can help you diffuse conflict with practicality. He can help the group concentrate on where they meet rather than focus on their differences. The stabilizing influence this has will help your group to regain its forward momentum.

Includer®
Those who have All Are Welcome Here doormats want everyone to be on the inside.

If you have a welcoming attitude, you accept a wide variety of people. You feel we are at our best when everyone is involved and working on a common goal. You believe all are equally important and you want to stretch the circle wider.

You can bring tolerance and acceptance to any gathering. Your hospitable nature makes you a natural at welcoming others. Your quickness to accept and invite others makes them feel valued for who they are.

When you want to ensure that your message is heard by diverse audiences, ask someone who is inclusive by nature to help. His ability to understand a wide variety of perspectives will help you enhance your communications and reach the broadest range of recipients.

Individualization®
The one who says, "You know what you would be good at?" can sense what is unique and different about people, what their preferences are, and what they do well. She sees every person as one of a kind.

If this sounds like you, you know that different people have different needs and you personalize your relationships with each. You want to give them what they need and appreciate most.

Your recognition of what is special about others draws out the best in them. You can find out what others do well and help them do it. By acknowledging differences, you can meet people where they're at and build their trust.

When you desire to help those on your team reach their goals, seek the input of someone who appreciates the uniqueness of people. She can use her ability to identify what is special about each person and serve as a casting director, helping you assign the roles that will bring out everyone's best performance.

Positivity®
Ever notice how some people seem to light up a room when they enter it? Their optimistic nature has a stimulating and confidence-building effect on others. Their sociability, warmth, and energy make others feel safe and supported. They are also giving us a clue that they are likely those who can live their values.

If this sounds like you, you are quick to smile, generous with praise, and love to laugh. Your contagious enthusiasm brings energy to any relationship or gathering. People want to be near you because their world looks better when you are around.

As you demonstrate your positive attitude, you inspire others to also look at the bright side. Sensing your optimism, they feel more hopeful.

When your team is feeling down, ask someone who is upbeat for some help. He can see what is right rather than what is wrong with a situation and can lighten the mood of the group. When the spirits of others are lifted a bit, they will be better able to focus on achieving results.

Relator®
The friend who looks in your eyes and says, "Tell me more" is likely one who has a close inner circle of friends and enjoys intense relationships with them. She is more interested in heartfelt and durable connections than in making casual acquaintances.

If this sounds like you, you value solid, genuine, and mutually rewarding relationships. You are drawn to people you already know and like to spend time with them. You purposefully encourage the deepening of select relationships and enjoy maintaining them. You enjoy quiet moments with people you deeply trust. As others see that you value true friendships and keep confidences, they perceive you as more trustworthy.

To sustain connection with those who are important to you, spend some one-on-one time with them. They will appreciate the effort and you will be fulfilled by the mutual sharing of feelings and experiences.

If you are involved in a project that will require a long-term commitment from the participants, consider enlisting someone who has deep relationships to join you. She will help you find the satisfaction that working hard with friends to achieve a goal can bring.

CHAPTER 4

Having a Positive Effect on Others

Respect People and Influence Them

with your Character Strengths[12]

FORGIVENESS®   HUMOR®   LEADERSHIP®

HUMILITY®   KINDNESS®

with your Work Strengths[13]

COMMUNICATION®   SELF ASSURANCE®   WOO®

DEVELOPER®   SIGNIFICANCE®

When you demonstrate that you care about others and are willing to help, it has a positive effect on them.

We'll address each of these 10 Having a Positive Effect on Others strengths with a look at:
- the signals it sends
- what it feels like
- how to use it
- engaging with others who have it

---

12 from the VIA Institute
13 from Gallup, Inc.

Using these strengths help you show others the concern you have for them and can prepare them to see the benefits of your perspectives.

HAVING A POSITIVE EFFECT ON OTHERS
WITH YOUR CHARACTER STRENGTHS

Forgiveness®

Those who refer to past injustices and slights to them as "water under the bridge" are demonstrating their signature strength of Forgiveness. Using this strength promotes equanimity between them and others. Forgiveness, the letting go of resentment, is closely related to mercy, the withholding of punishing people for their behavior. The USS Mercy and the USS Hope were big hospital ships in WWI and WWII. Our current hospital ships are the converted oil tankers USNS Mercy and USNS Comfort. A fine name for a companion ship would be the USNS Forgiveness. *That* would send a message.

When you forgive others, you telegraph that you can move on with your life after less-than-benevolent treatment from them. You overcome the negative emotion of resentment and are able to rise above minor offenses to you and maintain your healthy attitude.

Using your strength of Forgiveness to see others in a nonbinary way promotes calm in those around you. It is unlikely that anyone you know is a true 0 or a true 1. Most of us are somewhere near the golden mean, described by Aristotle as the desirable middle between two extremes. Remember that Forgiveness, the strength, is not tied to forgetfulness. Forgive *and* forget is not high-quality advice. When the distinctive black sedan with the aggressive driver behind the wheel cuts you off, let it go. The next time you see it coming up in your rearview mirror, be alert.

If you are feeling wobbly because of some minor wrongdoing by another, ask one with the Forgiveness strength to help you regain your balance. She can show you how to look at what happened and weigh the importance of this incident in the past and the benefit of your relationship with this person in the future.

Humility®

The one who lets his accomplishments speak for themselves is giving us a cue that he has the strength of Humility. Not only does he not *act* as if he is more special than others, he doesn't *feel* more special than others.

If this sounds like you, when the spotlight hits you, you move. Letting others have their turn is more important than bringing attention to yourself. It's not that you are shy or have a low opinion of yourself. Quite the opposite. A trait underlying the strength of Humility is healthy self-esteem.

Use your Humility to send the message that you are a modest person. Most people aren't crazy about braggarts, but almost everyone like those who are modest. Unless you are a popular recording artist singing some version of "Look at Me Now" in a Broadway musical, big budget film, or music video, most of us are attracted to those who do not draw too much attention to themselves.

If your strength of Humility is less than you would like it to be, ask someone with Humility as a signature strength how you can increase your own. His first bit of advice, simple but powerful, might be "listen more." Being a good listener, paying attention to what others are really saying, and complimenting them when appropriate, are some of the best ways to demonstrate that you want to have some humility in your humanity.

Humor®

Do you know someone who, when you see them, makes you smile? The likely cause is that they have Humor as a signature strength. Humor, constantly chipping away at unwarranted seriousness, prefers to take a lighter approach toward most things. The strength of Humor isn't about being the life of the party but, in most gatherings, we do notice that those with a sense of humor are ones who are socially attractive to others.

If this sounds like you, the contradictions in life amuse you and you are able to recognize absurdity when you see it.

There was this great guy in the risk management consulting firm I was with. He was always making little jokes. Some people found it distracting[14], but he was anything but distracted. He was whip smart and used his Humor to keep us from falling into personal pits as solemn as the issues we were considering. If you have some heavy stuff to deal with, ask someone with strong Humor to help you defuse the situation. A little bit of levity can work wonders.

Kindness®

Do you know someone who consistently "plays nice"? When he does so, his compassion and care for others has a positive effect on them. And he is demonstrating that he has Kindness among his signature strengths.

---

14 Yes, these were the humorless ones.

If this sounds like you, you enjoy doing little things for others. As Cliff Shaw, the systems programmer who developed the first AI program almost 70 years ago[15] said, "It's the little things, hundreds of 'em." Those hundreds of little things *you* do, they count. A lot. Can you imagine a world with too much kindness? Me neither.

Use your Kindness to show your awareness of others' needs. If you wish, let it remain your secret that you are the one who benefits most when you help them.

If the other party in one of your relationships is experiencing difficulties in his life, ask someone with Kindness as a signature strength to help you understand how you might assist your friend or coworker. He might be able to suggest just the right thing you can do that does not feel invasive to the person you are trying to help. Everyone appreciates Kindness, especially when they feel vulnerable.

Leadership®

If you don't know any natural-born leaders, maybe it's because there aren't any. Warren Bennis, who served on the faculties of Harvard and Boston University, discovered that leaders are made, not born.[16] And most leaders are self-made. This is good news for those of us who want to increase our strength of Leadership.

---

15 The Logic Theorist, a computer program, was cowritten in 1956 by Cliff Shaw, Alan Newell, and Herbert A. Simon at the RAND Corporation.
16 "The most dangerous leadership myth is that leaders are born—that there is a genetic factor to leadership. This myth asserts that people simply either have certain charismatic qualities or not. That's nonsense; in fact, the opposite is true. Leaders are made rather than born. And the way we become leaders is by learning about leadership through life and job experiences, not with university degrees," Warren Bennis, *Managing People Is Like Herding Cats* (Provo, UT: Executive Excellence Publishing, 1999), 163.

If you are one who is using and increasing your Leadership strength, you enjoy the challenge of bringing others together to get things done. Creating a vision, setting achievable goals, assembling work groups, keeping others' sense of fulfillment up, and accomplishing what you set out to do are rewarding activities.

Use your Leadership strength to organize and guide any effort that will benefit from having multiple participants work on a common goal. Whether it be in your community or in your profession, the world needs more leaders. There are positions open everywhere at every level. If you see an unfulfilled need for leadership somewhere, maybe you are the one who can fill it.

If you want to bring some people together who don't normally interact, ask someone with Leadership among his signature strengths to help you consider your options. He can familiarize you with the basic ingredients of leadership and the typical needs of followers. Then you will be on your way to improving your Leadership strength.

HAVING A POSITIVE EFFECT ON OTHERS WITH YOUR WORK STRENGTHS

Communication®
Do you know someone who has a way with words? Chances are he can put his thoughts and feelings into vivid word pictures that bring clarity and understanding to a topic.

If this sounds like you, you have an ability to express your thoughts in writing and speaking. You love to tell stories and make connections with others. You are a good listener and a good conversationalist. You can craft just the right message for any audience and can serve as an effective spokesperson for the ideas and opinions of others.

To use your strength of Communication, practice getting your message across. Find opportunities to think out loud, study the effect it has, then refine it. By doing so, you will improve your ability to capture the attention of others and be understood.

If you have a perplexing situation, invite in someone who is good at give-and-take conversations to help you talk through the options and bring what is being thought into words. This may provide you clarity on the issue so you can generate the dialogue that will help others find common ground.

Developer®
The ones who are always looking for ways to help people improve themselves love to develop others, inspiring and motivating them to become better versions of themselves.

If this sounds like you, you see what others can become. To you, people can realize their potential when they are provided the opportunities and encouragement to thrive. You feel everyone is on the path to getting better in some way. When you can participate in someone's process of improvement, you feel energized.

As you find ways people can improve themselves, you help them gain the most sustainable kind of forward motion—that which is generated internally.

When you or your team feel stalled on a project, someone who can see others' capacity to grow can bring hope to the process and serve as an energizing facilitator. He may reawaken you and your team members to your potential and inspire you to find new ways to experience success.

Self-Assurance®

Those who say, "We can *do* this!" are comfortable going first, will bravely lead the way, and will inspire others to trust them. Doing so, they can have a contagious effect on those around them, who also become more self-confident.

If this sounds like you, you deeply trust your instincts and are comfortable with your decisions. You are confident in your ability to live your own life. Your internal guidance system enables you to be independent and self-governing. You know you can take on challenges, address issues as they appear, and produce results.

Comfortable with risk, you use your intuition and certainty to bring a sense of order in times of chaos. Others appreciate the clarity and stability you bring to volatile situations.

During a complex project, if you find yourself at the marathon in the middle, where the way forward is not clear, invite someone with high Self-Assurance to join the effort. He will bring courage and a sense of certainty that will help you stay the course. His conviction that you are on the right path will encourage you and others to take initiative in a time of uncertainty.

Significance®

In 1998, Ford Motor Co. introduced, "Built to Last." Their powerful new slogan was all about the significance of their product and the durability of their legacy.

If you want to make a difference, you want to be recognized for doing work that is meaningful and of lasting value to others. You desire to be noticed, heard, and appreciated. You avoid unimportant tasks and spend your time doing the things that matter most. You feel a need to be admired as credible, professional, and successful.

Focus on making contributions that will have a positive effect on others. Your determination to make the world a better place inspires and motivates them to reach for outcomes they may not have considered.

If you associate with those who post noteworthy achievements, you will notice they are likely to be goal oriented. Acknowledge them for what they do well and the impact of their work. This will affirm their efforts and encourage them to make further contributions.

Woo®—"winning others over"

Ever notice how some people can start relationships and build rapport quickly and easily? They know how to form a positive connection with others by breaking the ice with a hearty welcome or melting it with their personal warmth.

If this sounds like you, you love meeting new people. You are charming, open, and create a space of social comfort for others.

When you transfer your enthusiasm to them, they feel included and more at ease.

Insert yourself into situations where you can be around people. It will energize you and give you opportunities to broaden your network. Volunteer to be a greeter at events of any kind. Your warmth and openness will make the attendees feel welcome.

When you need someone to help those at a gathering feel more at ease, enlist someone who enjoys meeting new people. She will be naturally hospitable and display a genuine interest in them. She will be able to quickly read people, engage them, and help them feel acknowledged and welcome.

CHAPTER 5

Performing with Excellence

Initiate Action and Carry Out Plans

with your Character Strengths[17]

BRAVERY®   PRUDENCE®   ZEST®

PERSEVERENCE®   SELF-REGULATION®

with your Work Strengths[18]

ACHIEVER®	COMPETITION®	MAXIMIZER®
ACTIVATOR®	CONSISTENCY®	RESPONSIBILITY®
ADAPTABILITY®	DELIBERATIVE®	RESTORATIVE®
ARRANGER®	DISCIPLINE®	
COMMAND®	FOCUS®	

When superior results are needed, these strengths will help you put your thoughts and plans into action.

We'll address each of these 18 Performing with Excellence strengths with a look at:

---

17 from the VIA Institute
18 from Gallup, Inc.

- the signals it sends
- what it feels like
- how to use it
- engaging with others who have it

Your Performing with Excellence strengths give you the stamina to stay on track and see significant projects through to their successful completion.

PERFORMING WITH EXCELLENCE WITH YOUR CHARACTER STRENGTHS

Bravery®

When King Henry implored, "Once more into the breach, dear friends, once more"[19] he was exhibiting just about all we need to know about the strength of Bravery.

If this sounds like something you would say, you see threats and opportunities as challenges and face them head on. Fear is something you can push through in service of reaching your personal goals or the shared goals of an organization you support.

Use your Bravery to subordinate fear to a level where you can objectively weigh the potential risks and rewards before you make a decision. Bravery is not the absence of fear. Rather, it is the willingness to act despite it. Some of the most decorated military pilots, praised for their heroism, have admitted they are frightened every time they get in a plane. Whether it is an external physical fear, fire for example, or an inner psychological

19 William Shakespeare, *Henry V*, 3.1.1. References are to act, scene, and line. Henry is rallying his troops to attack an enemy city through a gap in the wall that surrounds it.

one that is mental or emotional in nature, setting fear to the side for a while can help you see further down the road you are on.

Did you notice that we define bravery by squarely facing not only threats but opportunities? If you perceive something big may be coming your way, enlist the opinion of someone with Bravery to help you evaluate your options. It is human nature to become as paralyzed by big opportunities as it is by big perceived threats. Few of us can fly through the Alps in our wingsuits or lead high-tech startups into the unknown, but we can and should seize the opportunities we can take advantage of. Use Bravery to carpe *your* diems!

Perseverance®

When American journalist Jim Watkins said, "A river cuts through rock not because of its power, but because of its persistence," he was giving us a way to think about what we can achieve with the strength of Perseverance. People with Perseverance finish what they have started.

If *you* can cut through rock, you keep moving despite obstacles in your way. You stay the course. The grind of life? It gives you pleasure. You use your Perseverance to organize yourself so you can push on and see your projects through to completion.

Use your strength of Perseverance as the Energizer Bunny uses his batteries. They help him keep going, and going, and going...

When you are feeling a bit worn down by a journey you are on, ask someone with Perseverance among their signature strengths to help you consider what you can do to keep moving. You may see that focusing on small objectives, rather than your large goal, will give you the encouragement to regain some steady momentum and press forward.

Prudence®

When John Heywood wrote, "Look before you leap,"[20] he gave us an analogy to use the strength of Prudence to not take undue risks.

If you look before you leap, you are careful about the choices you make and can exhibit restraint in your life. Think of your Prudence as "wise caution."[21]

Engage your Prudence to govern yourself by the use of reason. Weigh the pluses and minuses of different thoughts, feelings, and actions to steer clear of avoidable mishaps in life. Examine the cost and benefit of each option you have before jumping headlong into something.

If the fast track you are on seems a bit too fast, ask one with Prudence as a signature strength to help you take the pace down a little. He can help you take a time-out to identify and avoid unnecessary risks and may encourage you to invoke the caution you will need to make prudent decisions.

---

20 The first English language version of this appeared in 1546, in a collection of proverbs produced by John Heywood, a musician and playwright in Tudor, England. In a few pages, you will see another one of the many translated by Heywood. Others include "a bird in the hand is worth two in the bush," "beggars can't be choosers," "let sleeping dogs lie," "the more the merrier," "can't see the forest for the trees," and another famous one that will appear in the next chapter.

21 Ryan M. Niemiec and Robert E. McGrath, *The Power of Character Strengths* (Cincinnati, OH: Via Institute on Character, 2019).

Self-Regulation®

When Lao Tzu said, "The best fighter is never angry,"[22] he was showing us one of the significant benefits of using our strength of Self-Regulation. A big part of the fun of life is our ability to make choices. We've all made some wise ones, and we've all made some stupid ones. Those who can use their strength of Self-Regulation are able to make the measured decisions that promote balance and order in their lives.

If you can activate your Self-Regulation, you can summon the self-control to delay or postpone gratification from tempting thoughts, feelings, and actions that do not serve you in achieving what is important to you.

Use your strength of Self-Regulation to manage potentially disruptive impulses and emotions. Self-Regulation is also a strength to call upon when deciding whether to approach or avoid

a concept	or	a way of thinking
an emotion	or	a way of feeling
an action	or	a way of acting.

To do so, gather your thoughts, feelings, and ways you naturally behave. Then consider how to best use them to reach your goals. Easy to say. Very hard to do without some Self-Regulation.

If you are engaged in an effort where you feel you are making too many decisions too quickly, ask one with Self-Regulation for assistance in charting your next steps. She may help you

---

22 c. 600 BC

see that, to act in your long-term self-interest, you will want to narrow your choices to the things that are consistent with your values. There are several sayings that speak to this. "An ounce of prevention, a pound of cure" and "measure twice, cut once" are two of the better ones.

Zest®

When Bertrand Russell said, "What hunger is in relation to food, zest is in relation to life," he was encouraging us to be enthusiastic and enjoy life whenever and wherever we can. He was urging us to unleash our strength of Zest.

If you are zestful, you willingly bring energy and excitement to the things you do. You feel alive and invigorated by the ideas you have, the people you know, and the projects you are committed to.

Use your strength of Zest to help you live a life that is meaningful and rewarding.

When you want to be more engaged in something, just add your strength of Zest to any desirable endeavor.

Desirable Endeavor + Zest = Engagement

Try this surefire shortcut when you want to jumpstart yourself to perform with excellence.

When you find yourself at a stage, as we all do at one time or another, where you dread getting out of bed and on with your day, ask someone with the signature strength of Zest to help you see things from a different perspective. He can help you focus on the positive aspects of your life. As you do so, you may be encouraged to do more of the activities that are desirable to you. Thinking and doing with some of your own Zest can reignite your enthusiasm and the vigor with which you can return to enjoying your life.

PERFORMING WITH EXCELLENCE WITH YOUR WORK STRENGTHS

Achiever®

When George Mallory, upon being asked why he was climbing Everest, said "because it is there,"[23] he was showing us in full color what Achiever the strength can help us attempt in life.

If this is you, you love your to-do lists. Every day presents new opportunities to accomplish new things. You take satisfaction in being busy and look forward to being productive in the hours ahead. You have an internal drive to finish and focus on completing what you have started.

You are a doer. Seek out collaboration partners who share your deep work ethic and durability. The more things you can achieve, the more satisfied you will be.

When you are feeling overwhelmed by the complexity of a project, ask someone who loves getting stuff done to help you. He can help you break down a goal into attainable tasks, inspiring you and others to complete them. His presence will strengthen your resolve to stay on track by addressing achievable objectives that move you toward the larger goal.

---

23 Often attributed to Edmund Hillary, who climbed Everest in 1953. Mallory was the one who first said this, before his fated attempt in 1924.

Activator®

When Mark Twain said, "The secret of getting ahead is getting started," he was raising our awareness that the cost of not getting going will be missed opportunities. Activators love to be in on the kickoff.

If this sounds like you, you make things happen by turning thoughts into action. You are always on the lookout for opportunities to move things forward and are good at identifying the best next steps. Your bias for acting, not thinking, makes you willing to take the risk to start something that hasn't been proven.

When others are stalled in their efforts, you can help them regain their momentum. When you do what you can to get the ball rolling, it will encourage others to break away from paralysis by analysis and inspire them to do something that will have a positive effect on one of their goals.

If your group gets stuck, one who is good at starting new things can bring you the courage to take the next step to get you back on your way again. His sense of urgency will inspire and mobilize others to act and create movement toward the goal.

Adaptability®

Some people are just better than the rest of us at playing whatever cards they are dealt in life. They live in the moment, love spontaneity, and thrive on variety. They accept interruptions and detours. They adapt to them with ease and can see the new opportunities they present.

If this sounds like you, you enjoy fluid environments and can respond quickly when the demands on you change. You live in the here and now and are comfortable with shifting situations and priorities.

In times of chaos or confusion, your flexibility helps you find opportunities to be productive. You can quickly survey a changing landscape and make the decisions that will lead to the best action right now.

If you are trying to sort out significant changes in your environment, ask someone who is adaptable for their perspective. He will be unruffled by the chaos, will be able to make some sense of it, and can help you adjust by focusing on the things that can be addressed now.

Arranger®

Imagine the maestro on his rostrum, the director of the big-budget movie, and the ringleader of the circus. In complex dynamic situations, they can see the best combination of all the variables and produce the optimum result with what is available at the time.

If this sounds like you, you see patterns and are always looking for the perfect configuration of people and resources to accomplish a new project or improve an existing one. You can evaluate the alternatives, devise new options, and discover the paths of least resistance. As you go about assembling the pieces of the puzzle, the picture that others can see and appreciate will emerge.

Volunteer for complex projects with opportunities to turn confusion into clarity. Sort through the clutter to find the straightest path forward. Search through the alternatives to discover the best ones. As you see where others excel and how they can achieve their optimal outcomes, they will appreciate your perspective and take comfort in the element of certainty it gives them.

In times of change, enlist someone who is good at seeing order in the chaos. He can be the calm in the eye of the storm as he arranges the ingredients into the best structure to deal with the uncertainty. This will help you allocate your personal resources and position the other team members where they will be most effective.

Command®

Whoever says "When the going gets tough, the tough get going" is one who, in uncertain times, can step in, take control of a situation, and make decisions. His Command strength enables him to take charge.

If this sounds like you, you are comfortable leading and making decisions. You bring control and order to situations and enjoy being in the driver's seat. You know when to go through a barrier rather than go around it. The strong presence you project inspires the confidence of others.

Exhibiting Command can bring clarity to ambiguous situations. Because you are undeterred by obstacles and don't shy away from conflict, you can be a persuasive presence. Your courage and decisiveness enable others to be less distracted and inspire them to align their actions with the broader goals.

74

When a group you belong to needs stronger leadership, consider enlisting someone who shares or understands your values, vision, and goals and enjoys being in charge of things. He can ask the questions that need to be asked, say what needs to be said, and may be the right one to lead the group in a way that will help it regain its forward progress.

Competition®

Those who are "in it to win it" are invigorated by competing. With no interest in participant ribbons, they thrive on winning.

If this sounds like you, you are intensely aware of the performance of others and measure your progress against them. The nature of competition is two parties striving for a goal that cannot be shared. If you can compete, you can win. If you can win, you can celebrate.

Find a way to have a small win every day. Try to do something better than someone who is a worthy opponent. Competing purposefully will help you keep your edge sharp.

If you are uncertain about your ability to beat rivals in a contest, enlist someone who enjoys meeting challenges from rivals. He will be able to help you evaluate each competitor and how to best them. This will enable you to form a game plan and prepare in a way that will set you up for a win.

Consistency®

When Thomas Jefferson began the Declaration of Independence with, "We hold these truths to be self-evident, that all men are created equal," he was introducing the guiding hand of constancy into a time of uncertainty. His belief that people function best in an environment where the rules are clear and applied to everyone equally, had as its goal the creation of a stable society that would be predictable and evenhanded.

If this sounds like you, you are keenly aware of the need to treat everyone similarly. You know that rules keep us safe and that the playing field must be a level one. You are able to make decisions that are fair and equitable for all. As you do so, your predictability aids stability. As a result, people see you as trustworthy.

Repeat the processes that have been proven to work and be on the lookout for future routines that will improve your performance. Help others explore their existing options before creating custom solutions.

During rapid change, when people are unclear about the rules, someone who exhibits steadiness and dependability can bring clarity. She will be able to identify the proven approaches that will continue to work in the future. Her consistent approach to things will provide a sense of safety. By helping others see what *isn't* changing, she will enable them to navigate the waters of uncertainty.

Deliberative®
When John Heywood wrote "Haste makes waste,"[24] he put voice to how we can increase our productivity by taking the time to be thorough.

---

24 In his 1546 collection of proverbs

If you are a careful person, you think before you act and you execute with caution. You sort through the options, anticipate obstacles, and assess the risks. After thorough consideration of each course of action, you make your decision and proceed with certainty.

As you consider the alternatives, draw upon prior experiences when you accurately anticipated what could go wrong. Introduce your thoughtful process to those looking for the best way to execute. Your ability to identify the potential for future mistakes can help others produce high-quality results in a way that minimizes risk.

If you are working on a project with many variables and feel as if you are entering a minefield, enlist someone who takes care in making their decisions to help you execute in the most considered way. He will help you carefully evaluate the options before you make your next step.

Discipline®

Someone who believes in the message, "plan your work and work your plan and you will be a wealthy man" achieves results by working through all the steps necessary to reach the goal.

If this sounds like you, you enjoy routines and structure. You like things to be predictable and planned. You want to accomplish tasks in the most orderly and effective way. When you identify a destination, you form a process and diligently follow a prescribed route and method to get yourself there. To achieve your desired result, you thoughtfully move through the steps in an orderly fashion.

Fine-tune your systems and share them with others. Volunteer to be the one who oversees the action plan. You can contribute orderliness to the process and to the lives of others who are involved.

When one of your projects can benefit from a more methodical approach, engage with one who can exhibit control and restraint. He can help you work through the options one step at a time and stay the course. This will provide you and others with a sense of safety and order.

Focus®

The one who reminds us to "keep your eye on the ball" is telling us we are more likely to accomplish something if we concentrate on it while we are attempting to do it.

If you can keep *your* eye on the ball, you set goals and confine your actions to those that will help you achieve the desired results. You stay on the most direct path and avoid distractions. Your goals serve as your compass, pointing you toward the places where you are needed. You instinctively evaluate the actions that will move you toward your objective.

Use your Focus to concentrate on one task at a time and stick with it until it is complete. Others will appreciate your ability to limit distractions and direct your attention to the most important issues.

Is one of your projects getting off track? Engage someone with a high ability to concentrate to help you lead by example. His work ethic and dedication to the goal will reduce the distractions for others and help them to prioritize effectively. As they do so, they will experience a sense of clarity and purpose.

Maximizer®

The ones who swing for the fences are all about the pursuit of perfection. They set and reach stretch goals and encourage others to do the same.[25]

If this sounds like you, you focus on quality and strive for excellence. Rather than fix what is broken, you apply yourself to efforts that will produce a significant return on investment. You like to be around other high performers and thrive when taking things from good to great.

Be selective about what you seek to improve. Invest yourself in endeavors that have the highest potential to further your purpose. Consider what is most important and do everything you can to improve the odds for a favorable outcome. Give yourself a timeline so you know when to call it done. Offer to help others who are looking to make things better in their lives.

When you are in the final stages of a project, ask the opinion of someone who has a "whatever it takes" attitude. He will bring a sense of abundance to the process, and you may discover ways in which your project can be improved. This will inspire you and others to achieve the best results you are capable of.

---

25 My wife and I both have Maximizer among our signature strengths. We laugh that our family motto is WIT—"whatever it takes." All we need now is some high falutin' family crest with the unproduceable Latin translation "quicquid capit" below in a fancy scroll.

Responsibility®
When Carl Jung said, "You are what you do, not what you say you'll do," he was referring to those who can be counted upon to fulfill the promises they make. When they say they will do something, they mean it.

If this sounds like you, you are diligent and dependable, a promise-keeper. You are conscientious about meeting your obligations and stick with your projects until completion. You have a deep sense of dedication and ownership of your responsibilities. You take seriously the commitments you make to yourself and others. This inspires others to trust you and depend upon you.

Be selective about your commitments. Volunteer yourself only for work that is worthy of your efforts and that you can do well.

In times of change, someone with a sense of ownership can bring great stability to partnerships. He can be the voice to recap what has been accomplished, illuminate what needs to be finished before starting something new, and review what everyone agreed upon at the start. This will help others avoid distractions and work on what was promised.

Restorative®
He who says, "We can fix this!" views broken as a temporary state. He brings reassurance that things aren't so far gone that the pieces cannot be mended and put back in place.

If this sounds like you, you have a drive to solve problems and like to fix things that need repair. You can identify the underlying factors that led to the damage. You use existing resources to address the issues and have the tenacity to stay with solving the problem until the solution is found. You are a valued resource to others who need a collaborator to help them get back on track.

You enjoy working on problems where you can return something to its best working order. Your ability to see what can be saved and fixed can be valuable in turnaround situations. When you spot possible future problems, share your insights with others. This will enable them to see how the damage can be avoided.

In times of crisis, include someone who likes to fix things to help you see how order can be restored. He can help you identify where things went wrong and how they might be fixed. As you begin the repair process, it will encourage others to fix problems rather than circumvent them. This can improve morale and the situation at large.

CHAPTER 6

Aligning to Your Values

Practice Self-Awareness and Self-Care

with your Character Strengths[26]

APPRECIATION OF BEAUTY AND EXCELLENCE®

GRATITUDE® **SPIRITUALITY®**

HOPE®

with your Work Strengths[27]

BELIEF® **CONNECTEDNESS®**

The strengths that help us to be self-aware can enhance our understanding of our most important values and needs. The strengths that help us practice self-care are the ones we use to act on what we believe and sustain our mental, emotional, and physical health.

We'll address each of these six Aligning to Your Values strengths with a look at:

- the signals it sends
- what it feels like

---

26 From the VIA Institute
27 From Gallup, Inc.

- how to use it
- engaging with others who have it

These strengths can provide deep support for your personal development.

ALIGNING TO YOUR VALUES USING YOUR CHARACTER STRENGTHS

Appreciation of Beauty and Excellence®
When Thomas Aquinas said, "One will observe that all things are arranged according to their degrees of beauty and excellence,"[28] he was making the case that beautiful and excellent things are superior to those that are not. In his time, around 1250, when beautiful and excellent things were relatively rare, Aquinas correlated them with heaven. Fast forward to today. Now, when beauty and excellence are accessible to most of us, we correlate them with happiness,[29] our heaven on earth.

If what Thomas Aquinas said sounds like something you would say, you have deep feelings for and experience close relationships with concepts, things, experiences, and people that strike you as beautiful or exceptional in some way. You take delight in

---

28 c. 1250. Aquinas was a priest and a philosopher in medieval Italy. In his time, the earth's population was around 400 million—it is 7.5 billion today—and life was a hard and brutish affair for most, with scant opportunities to witness much beauty or excellence.

29 For your amusement: In the November 2013 issue of the *European Economic Review* is an article titled "Beauty Is the Promise of Happiness?" (The title refers to the quote "Beauty is the promise of happiness," attributed to the French writer with the pen name Stendhal in 1822.) The article closes with this notation: "The authors are listed in ascending order of their looks" The things you can find on the internet!

appreciating the wonders of nature, mathematics and science, the arts, and the characteristics and achievements of others. In the presence of them, you feel awe and the inspiration to make your own contributions to the beauty and excellence in the world.

Use your Appreciation of Beauty and Excellence to bring yourself closer to the ideas, things, and people that align with your values. When you sense the onset of mental or emotional numbness from performing routine tasks, take a break. Think about a few of your values. Then walk outside or look out of a different window and identify some things or people that appear to align with these values. If you look, you will find them. Once you start seeing them, you will more easily be able to find new ones every time you repeat the exercise. Recognizing the beauty around you and the excellence of other people can have a refreshing effect.

If you are feeling your horizon could use some expanding, ask someone with the strength Appreciation for Beauty and Excellence to spend some time with you. Go for coffee, duck into a museum or church, sit on a park bench, or just listen to some music. Ask them what they see and hear. Soon, you will begin to see and hear new examples of beauty and excellence that are attractive to you. Think about how these relate to your values. On another day, try to find some more.

Gratitude®
Those who "realize how blessed we are" are always ready to show appreciation for the good things in the world and for that which they have received. When they do so, they give us a glimpse into the strength of Gratitude.

If this sounds like you, you are thankful for many things in your life—a smile from a child, a beautiful sunset, a thoughtful gift from a friend, and the opportunity to do your best at work. Many people will want to think a bit before they name what they are grateful for. You can readily produce a list and take pleasure in doing so. You will probably precede it by saying, "Thank you for asking."

Gratitude has long been a tenet of religion. It is only recently, within the last 20 years or so, that it has become a subject of systemic study in the field of psychology. As a result, we now know much more about how to use our strength of Gratitude in ways that will benefit ourselves and others. Use your Gratitude to express thanks for what you value. Let others know how much you appreciate their presence in your life, use your appreciation for what you hold dear to cheer yourself up, and be thankful for some of the good things you take for granted.

The next time you are feeling like an ungrateful wretch, ask someone with Gratitude among their signature strengths to help you get out of your ditch. She may divert your attention from what is unattractive and unjust in your life to some things you can be thankful for. Chances are, there are many more things you can appreciate than things you can disparage. Then you can say, "Thanks, Gratitude...I needed that!"

Hope®
Whoever first said, "Hope is praying for rain, but faith is bringing an umbrella" was illustrating how the strength of Hope promotes positive expectations that can lead to confident optimism.

If you are hopeful, you have a desire and an expectation that good things will happen. Your strength of Hope propels you to achieve your goals and supports you emotionally. While others may focus on the downsides and uncertain or negative consequences of their actions, your hopefulness gives you the positive attitude that carries you through life's little inconveniences. As a result, you are seldom anxious or depressed.

Use your commitment to your values and your strength of Hope to persevere when facing a significant challenge. There will be times when you will be unable to come up with a tidy solution to a dilemma. Hope to the rescue. Trust what you believe in, be optimistic, and give the good things in your life a chance to happen by *wanting* them to happen.

If you find yourself doing all the right things but are not seeing the results you desire, talk with someone who has Hope among her signature strengths. She may validate that what you are trying to accomplish has merit and the way you are going about it is the right way. Summoning John Heywood again, "Rome wasn't built in a day." As she gives you some of her hopefulness, she can provide you comfort that you are on the right track and are moving toward your goal.

Spirituality®

Do you know people who feel connected to something bigger than themselves? If so, you are fortunate to know some who are spiritual. They may have the strength of Spirituality in the traditional religious sense, or they may have it in the more contemporary "deepest meanings and values by which people live"[30] sense.

---

30 Philip Sheldrake, *A Brief History of Spirituality* (Hoboken, NJ: Wiley-Blackwell, 2007); David Ray Griffin, Spirituality and Society (Albany, NY: State University of New York Press, 1988)

If you are one of them, your strength of Spirituality supports your feeling that we are all connected by something beyond the known and observable realm. If you are religious, your portals to that dimension may be the Scriptures and the values they espouse. If you believe in a force that unites us all to one another, your portals to that dimension may be your own values. Whether your preference is one or the other or a combination of both, you feel grounded by unseen things that give your life a sense of purpose.

Use your Spirituality to find your reason for being, and to live your life in a way that gives you the highest sense of purpose. The word spirituality means different things to different people. The best meaning of it for you is what you *want* it to mean. Whatever your definition, use your strength of Spirituality to see your "place in the grand scheme of things and find meaning in everyday life."[31]

When you are feeling adrift, disconnected, and in need of a virtual mother ship, talk with a few friends who have different ways of demonstrating their spiritual strength. When you consider the deep connections they feel and how they use them to live happier more productive lives, you may be inspired to strengthen your link to something that is bigger and better than any of us.

31 Ryan M. Niemiec and Robert E. McGrath, *The Power of Character Strengths* (Cincinnati, OH: Via Institute on Character, 2019), 268.

ALIGNING TO YOUR VALUES USING YOUR WORK STRENGTHS

Belief®

Those who "do the right thing" possess a sense of right and wrong that drives how they act. Situational ethics are for others. These folks have deeply held ideals and can be depended upon to uphold their standards. When they do so and live according to their values, we view them as dependable and trustworthy.

If this sounds like you, your core values give your life meaning and a sense of purpose. Your motivation, drive, and determination come from living your life according to your convictions. Your values drive you to execute. The most important aspect of your life is staying true to them.

Align the work you do with your values and your purpose. Engage with organizations whose missions line up with your ideals. Build trust by communicating what you find important and share your passion with others. Show compassion by respecting the values they hold dear.

During times of change in an organization, one with strong convictions can be the compass that helps people remember they are remaining true to the cause and that their work is important. The clarity those with Belief provide can bring a sense of stability and inspire hope.

Connectedness®

Those who consider fate to be inevitable know that nothing happens by chance. Like Isaac Newton, they see that for every action, there will be an equal and opposite reaction—that the things we experience are somehow connected to other things.

89

If this sounds like you, you sense that we are all part of a bigger whole. You are fascinated by the links between people, ideas, and events. You can see how the little things in the past and present may become part of the future.

Use your sense of coherence to help others take a broader perspective and find meaning in their lives. Encourage them to step back and see the connections that run through everyday circumstances.

In times of instability or when you are experiencing overwhelm, enlist the views of someone who sees the world as a cohesive place. She can bring a sense of calm to the confusion and help you see how things are connected. As she does so, you will begin to understand that where you have been can lead you to somewhere better. As you do so, you may also begin to see where you can build bridges between other people and ideas.

PART II

The Competencies

These Make You Exceptional

*The answer to "What makes a leader exceptional?" is simple:
competencies.*
—Carson Dye & Andrew N. Garman, *Exceptional Leadership*[32]

In this section, we introduce the Level Up Competencies.

The current competency movement began in the 1970s with the studies of David McClelland, a Harvard psychology professor. He argued that intelligence tests were not all that valid and that grades did not predict success in real life. He proposed these traditional forms of assessment be abandoned and replaced with a better methodology, which he labeled "competencies." He defined *competencies* as:

The underlying characteristics of people, which enables them to deliver superior performance in a given job, role, or situation.

A year after the Enron fiasco, Malcolm Gladwell, in his famous *New Yorker* article about Enron's relationship with consulting firm McKinsey & Company, noted that,

---

32 Carson Dye and Andrew N. Garman, *Exceptional Leadership*, (Chicago: Health Administration Press, 2006).

> The link between IQ and job performance is distinctly underwhelming. On a scale where 0.1 or below means virtually no correlation and 0.7 or above implies a strong correlation (your height, for example, has a 0.7 correlation with your parents' height), the correlation between IQ and occupational success is between 0.2 and 0.3.[33]

His point was that success in school comes from working alone. But success in the real world comes from your ability to work with others.

It is by use of our competencies that we can make a difference, a contribution in the world.

Seth Godin notes,

> Big ideas, generous work, important breakthroughs— to pursue these goals is to abandon the metric of the moment in favor of a more useful sort of contribution. If we want smart kids, the GPA is a lousy way to get them.[34]

If the concept of competencies is newish to you, you may be asking,

WHY COMPETENCIES?

Aren't our strengths enough?

One of the great things about our strengths is that they are multidirectional. They can go anywhere at any time and their bags are always packed.

33 Malcolm Gladwell, "The Talent Myth," *New Yorker*, July 22, 2002.
34 Seth's Blog, "The Irony of Close Competition," July 6, 2019, https://seths.blog/2019/07/the-irony-of-close-competition.

But how do we engage our strengths to help us accomplish something specific?

That's what competencies are for.

Competencies serve as the conduits to focus our strengths and energies on our objectives with a precision that will help us achieve our desired results.

As our strengths describe HOW we can think, feel, and act, our competencies describe WHAT we can do with them.

To illustrate, let's imagine some situations where you use a strength exclusively versus a strength in support of a competency.

Situation	Only a strength	A competency-strength combo
Reception	*Woo* Walk in the room, turn on the charm.	*Build Collaborative Relationships-Woo* Use your time productively by making a good first impression on someone you wish to work with. Engage your Woo to start the relationship off on a friendly note.
	Social Intelligence Walk in the room, objectively sense the feelings and motives of others.	*Build Collaborative Relationships-Social Intelligence* Use your emotional intelligence to consider aspects about someone you wish to work with before you engage him in conversation. Use Social Intelligence to lay a foundation upon which you can create a productive relationship.
Team stalled	*Activator* Do something, anything, now.	*Managing Conflict-Activator* Take that difficult first step to address the cause of the stoppage—a conflict between two members of the team.

	Leadership Remain positive and dedicated to achieving the goal.	*Managing Conflict-Leadership* Consider reorganizing the team in a small way that will better the team's chances to move forward and will encourage them to do so.
Rapid Change	*Command* You've got this, now run with it.	*Communicating-Command* Create a sense of stability during a time of uncertainty by leading a discussion on the change in a confident manner.
	Bravery Meet the change head on.	*Communicating-Bravery* Let others know you share their concern for the challenges, threats, and difficulties ahead and that you are committed to finding the best possible approach to each one.

We are more effective when we use our strengths to support our competencies. Can you see how the competency focuses the strengths to do the most good and magnifies the beneficial effect the strength can have?

This is the reason why, as adults, it's usually better to be defined by our specific capabilities—our competencies—than to be announced by the general areas in which we have potential—our strengths.

FROM COMPETENT TO CAPABLE

With the Level Up Method, we use our competencies as vehicles to carry our strengths to achieve specific objectives.

Our competencies give us a way to put our plans into action, achieve our goals, and become more capable. Who doesn't want to be considered capable? But what is the difference between being competent and being capable?

| Competency | The ability to perform at high levels |
| Capability | The capacity to use competencies in creative and useful ways in new situations |

Another comparison:

Competence is an essential ingredient of being capable.[35]

The Level Up Competencies are the ones most useful to achieving the results that look like success. There are 5 categories of competencies and 17 distinct competencies within the 5 categories.

The 5 Categories of Competencies

THINKING STRATEGICALLY
NAVIGATING CHANGE
LEADING PEOPLE
DRIVING RESULTS
DEVELOPING SELF

Strengths alone are not always enough to achieve a desired goal. But when fitted to a competency, our strengths are terrific drivers toward our goals.

Applying our strengths to our competencies,
we enhance our capability.

As you create and practice your competency-strength combos, you will assemble your own unique Constellation of Competencies on which you can depend to help you to make meaningful progress

---

35 R. Nagarajan and R. Prabhu, "Competence and Capability—A New Look," *International Journal of Management Reviews* 6, no. 6 (June 6, 2015): 7–11.

when facing specific situations. One competency does not make us capable, but a constellation of them does.

Another benefit of using your competency-strength combinations to initiate your thoughts and actions is that you can *introduce your strengths before they introduce you.*

The BIG IDEA of Part II:

Competencies help us achieve our objectives. We can improve our competencies by intentionally selecting the strengths that will best help us use our competencies to produce the results we desire.

To achieve an
OBJECTIVE

+

select the
COMPETENCY
that will be most effective

+

support it with the
STRENGTH
that will most increase the competency's power.

+

Use this
COMPETENCY-STRENGTH COMBINATION
to

=

produce
RESULTS

As we investigate each competency in the coming chapters, consider how your signature character and work strengths might best support it. As you harness your strengths to improve your competencies, you will be on your way to developing the best possible version of you.

Remember how some of our strengths can be "free-range" and serve in one or more of our Sets of Strengths? For each of the 17 competencies, we will give you examples of how you might use a character strength or a work strength to improve the competency. Note that each strength is featured but once in these illustrations. The strengths that will best help you improve a competency will depend upon on what your signature strengths are and how you can use them to enhance the competency.

The folks at the top of your industry, the ones who make success seem effortless? They have mastered the art of applying their strengths to the competencies that help them achieve their intended outcomes in the most efficient manner. Improving and exercising our competencies are essential to success.

Every segment of the arts, sciences, business, and athletics has its own subset of competencies—the ones that will support achievements in a specific area. Our list of competencies includes the ones most beneficial to high achievers, leaders, and high potentials in all fields.

Next up are the 17 competencies you can use to achieve almost any goal. First, a word about the order in which they are presented. When you see the list for the first time, note that most competencies are additive; their categories start with "above, and..." This means that the preceding competencies prepare you for improving the ones that follow. As we make our way through the competencies, you will see how this works.

Here now, the competencies...

THE 17 COMPETENCIES IN THEIR 5 CATEGORIES

1   Thinking Strategically
        Creating Vision
        Making Decisions
        Developing Plans

2   Navigating Change
            above, and...
        Tolerating Risk
        Negotiating
        Communicating Clearly

3   Leading People
            above, and...
        Building Collaborative Relationships
        Inspiring Others
        Developing Others
        Influencing Others
        Leading Teams
        Managing Conflict

4   Driving Results
            above, and...
        Taking Initiative
        Executing Efficiently

5   Developing Self
        Continually Learning
        Acting Professionally
        Continuously Improving

THE STRENGTH-COMPETENCY-ACHIEVEMENT MODEL
HOW WE AND OTHERS PERCEIVE OUR VALUE

Here is a graphic to visualize how the Level Up Competencies focus and transmit our strengths to our objectives, and how we and others perceive our achievements.

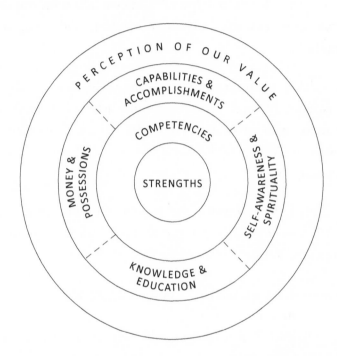

In the center are our signature strengths. Surrounding them are the 17 competencies. The middle ring consists of four general categories of achievements commonly used to describe success in ourselves or others.[36] The outer ring is our perception of our worth and others' perception of our value.

---

36 Success is not perfection. One of the features that makes life so interesting is its chaotic nature, so nothing will ever be perfect. "*Success is relative. It is what we make of the mess we have made of things.*" -T.S. Eliot

We work *in to out*, using our strengths to support the competencies best suited to achieving our goals and moving toward our vision. As we do so, we collect valuable experiences and produce a variety of achievements.

Others see us from *out to in*, first noticing our accomplishments. If they wish to better understand us, they might speculate about the competencies we used to achieve our results and our signature strengths.

In Level Up, we primarily refer to improving our Capabilities and Accomplishments. But we can also use our strengths and competencies to produce the other achievements: Education and Knowledge, Money and Possessions, and Self-Awareness and Spirituality.

The dotted lines between the segments in the achievement ring are to acknowledge that our accomplishments can migrate between the four sections:

- The right kind of Education might be a real Accomplishment.
- Useful Knowledge will help you increase your Capabilities.
- Self-Awareness will help you be more Capable.
- Commercially valuable Capabilities and Accomplishments can increase your Money and Possessions.
- Spirituality can increase your Capabilities in several areas.

If this were a physical model, in the central Strengths section would be a pizza of your six or so signature character strengths and nine or so signature work strengths. The next ring would have 17 sections, one for each competency. By rotating the Competencies ring and the achievements ring, you could "dial in" and align the best competency-strength combo with what you hope to accomplish in the achievements ring.

SOME CLARITY ON COMPETENCIES

This book is for the high achiever and the high potential who are seeking to level up, professionally and personally. If this is you, you are likely already leading others or on the leadership path. As a leader, you do not need to be a master of all the competencies, but you will want to be functional in most of the five categories of competencies. The rest of us, less concerned with the goals of others, can focus our attention on the competencies best suited for our personal objectives.

You may be wondering, "Why are we investing so much in developing our competencies?"

The frank answer is, "Because competent people are more productive than incompetent ones."

Fortunately, applying nearly *any* strength to *any* competency will result in greater competence.

This means, regardless of your signature strengths, you can develop any and all these competencies with them. You can be wildly successful and still be completely yourself.

In fact, using the strengths you have developed to become more competent is downright enjoyable. More on this soon, when we get to the passage on flow.

Ours is not a complete list of all competencies. The closest thing would be the US Office of Personnel Management (OPM)'s MOSAIC system. It lists the competencies needed to perform successfully in 200 federal occupations. Twenty-six of them begin with A. Unless you are an HR professional, you do not want to see this list.

Why don't we include subject matter and industry knowledge among our competencies to achieve success? Because these are table stakes to get in the game, and you are already in the game. To consistently achieve at a high level, your competencies in Thinking Strategically, Leading Change, Leading People, Driving Results, and Developing Self are more important than functional expertise.

As your competencies improve and increase in number, so will your self-confidence. Confidence is a key ingredient of living a rewarding life. Having confidence promotes a sense of optimism and calm within you.

Indeed,

> *competency-strength combinations are the ultimate confidence builders.*

Competence and confidence make a powerful blend. Others will sense it and respond favorably, assisting you to get to where you most want to go in life.

WOVEN COMPETENCIES: YOUR CONSTELLATION OF COMPETENCIES

In the chapters that follow, you will see how to use your signature strengths to develop your own powerful competency-strength combinations.

After you use a combo successfully a few times, the competency and the strength will weave themselves together into one. Your strength will become part of the competency, and your competency will improve the value of your strength.

We call these your woven competencies. Very potent, they are the ones that will comprise your own personal *Constellation of Competencies.* You own them, they define you, and they will be among the most effective capabilities in your repertoire.

In the four stages of learning any new skill, called the *Four Stages of Competence,* the highest level we can achieve is that of Unconscious Competence.[37] This is what your woven competencies become.

---

37 Introduced by Noel Burch, of Gordon International, in the 1970s.

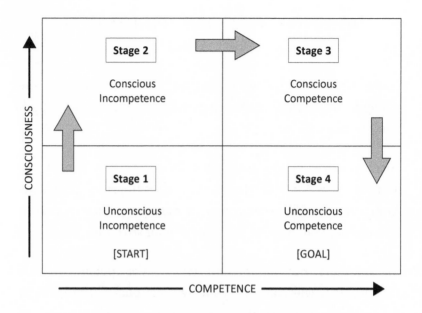

You may have come to this book knowing you could get better and wanting to do something about it. If so, your Level Up journey began at Stage 2: Conscious Incompetence. As you come to understand and practice competency-strength combos, you progress to Stage 3: Conscious Competence. You can do it, but you have to think about it, like a child moving his lips when he is learning how to read. When you've successfully used a combo a few times, the strength and competency become woven together and you can activate it to achieve things quickly. That's Stage 4: Unconscious Competence.

Consider Communicating Clearly, a competency each of us uses frequently. Two diverse strengths that bind easily into Communicating Clearly are Empathy and Command. Imagine someone with signature Empathy, then someone with signature Command. Can they use their strengths to communicate effectively? Yes, they can. Empathic communications are one thing, commanding communications quite another. Both are useful ways to communicate deeply and to accomplish different results in very different ways. What powerful woven competencies Communicating Clearly-Empathy and Communicating Clearly-Command can be.

WOVEN COMPETENCIES: YOUR GATEWAY TO FLOW

Your woven competencies differentiate you. And you own them. When a challenge presents itself, you intuitively know which to summon and how to best apply it. When you use your woven competencies to solve worthy goals, you feel energized and completely focused. Time stands still; nothing else seems to matter. Thanks to Hungarian-American psychologist Mihaly Csikszentmihalyi,[38] there is a name for this phenomenon—*flow*—and many insights into the nature of it.

When we are in flow, he observes, we are in a state of complete concentration and absorption in an activity. And "we're most likely to enter into that state of total work immersion when the challenge of the task is roughly equal to our ability to compete it."[39]

In flow, we are in the zone. Here's a great account from Bill Russell, legendary center for the Boston Celtics:[40]

---

38 "CHICK-sent-me-high-ee"
39 Mihaly Csikszentmihalyi, *Flow: The Psychology of Optimal Experience*, (New York: Harper Perennial Modern Classics, 2008).
40 William F. Russell, *Second Wind: The Memoirs of an Opinionated Man* (New York: Simon & Shuster, 1991).

> *It was almost as if we were playing in slow motion.*
> *During those spells I could almost sense how the next*
> *play would develop*
> *and where the next shot would be taken.*

As a leader, high achiever, or high potential, you want to maximize the likelihood of flow in your life. How to do so? Develop your woven competencies, apply them to worthy goals, and *you* will be in the zone.

How to know when we are in a state of flow? It feels like this:

1 Completely involved in what we are doing—focused, concentrated
2 A sense of ecstasy—being outside everyday reality
3 Great inner clarity—knowing what needs to be done and how well we are doing
4 Knowing the activity is doable—that our skills are adequate to the task
5 A sense of serenity—no worries about oneself and a feeling of growing beyond the boundaries of the ego
6 Timelessness—thoroughly focused on the present, hours seem to pass by in minutes
7 Intrinsic motivation—whatever produces flow becomes its own reward[41]

My memories of being in flow range from running my little lemonade stand when I was a kid, to working with the leadership team of a large tech client to solve a sticky problem.

---

41 Mihaly Csikszentmihalyi, "Flow: The Secret to Happiness," TED Talk, 2004.

THE COMPETENCY—FLOW—HAPPINESS LINK

Can you think of instances when you were in flow—when you knew what to do, did it, and the time flew by? You may not have been aware of it at the time, but chances are you were engaging your woven competencies. And you were happy. Csikszentmihalyi discovered that the happiest people are the ones who spend the most time in flow, when they are engaged in reaching their goals. He also found that happiness is an activity, not a fixed state, and can be developed as we learn to achieve flow in our lives.

How do we achieve flow in our lives?

Csikszentmihalyi identifies three necessary ingredients:

1 Balance of high competencies and challenge
2 Concentration
3 Immediate feedback and constant goal awareness

Increased productivity, flow, and the potential for happiness—three wonderful benefits will come from using your competency-strength combos to achieve your goals.

Like this:

As you become more productive, you will also gain access to new opportunities and be difficult for others to imitate. Your competencies will differentiate you as unique and valuable.

STILL FEELING YACHTY?

To your strengths, which you can use

- as an ANCHOR when you need to hold your position
- as a RUDDER when you need to change direction
- as an ENGINE to provide forward momentum from within
- as a SAIL to leverage your environment and propel you forward

We now introduce the competencies, to serve

- as the SHIP'S WHEEL to point your strengths in the right direction
- as a KEEL to help you maintain your heading

Your understanding of your unique strengths prepared you for the next step—to select the competencies that will help you accomplish your goals. Each of the following five chapters is devoted to a category of competency and the specific competencies within the category.

Now, let's explore how you can develop the competencies that will enable you to reach your goals and enjoy the process as you do so.

CHAPTER 7

Thinking Strategically

Shaping the Future

Hope is not a strategy.
—Vince Lombardi

Strengths is a strategy.
—Gallup

CREATING VISION
MAKING DECISIONS
DEVELOPING PLANS

When you improve your competencies within Thinking Strategically, you shape a desirable and attainable future, then plot the best course to take you there. Thinking Strategically is the critical first step in preparing to be the best possible version of you. This is where you evaluate your options and form the plans that will get you where you want to go. Thinking Strategically is being *proactive*, creating the future you wish, rather than being *reactive*, responding to what life hands you and hoping for the best.

Thinking strategically sets the stage for you to *act* strategically. The three Thinking Strategically competencies lay the foundation for the three categories of our acting competencies that follow: Navigating Change, Leading People, and Driving Results.

Thinking Strategically: the Competencies
versus
Thinking Thoroughly: the Strengths

Some clarification on Thinking Strategically, this category of three competencies, and Thinking Thoroughly, the set of thirteen strengths:

Competencies are *what* make us exceptional

Using our Strengths is *how* we develop them in our own unique way

Yes, some of the strengths you will use in the Thinking Strategically category of competencies will be those from the Thinking Thoroughly set of strengths. To be fully functional at Thinking Strategically, you will also want to engage your strengths from the Interacting with Others, Having a Positive Effect on Others, and Performing with Excellence sets.

I will provide plenty of examples to show you how different strengths can be used to support different competencies. For the scope of this chapter, we'll break down each of the Thinking Strategically competencies and provide suggestions on:

- What the competency is,
- Why this competency is valuable,
- What the competency looks like in action, and
- How to use your strengths to improve this competency in a way that is uniquely suited to you and your success.

CREATING VISION

The only thing worse than being blind is having sight but no vision.
—Helen Keller

Your mental image of what you can and want to be? That's your vision.

When you were a child, your vision was what you wanted to be when you grew up.

Maybe you wanted to ride horses. Or fly airplanes. Or have fancy parties. Or cure cancer. Or celebrate your Nobel Prize for curing cancer while riding your pony at a fancy party on your private jet. Very likely, you played games or read books that made that vision feel more real to you.

As adults, we have adjusted and refined the dreams of our childhood. Still, our mental image of what we can and want to be gives us a sense of destination. We use it to stay focused on our dreams and act with intention.

Timothy Gallwey, author of the popular Inner Game series sums it up, "If you have a clear vision of where you want to go, you are not as easily distracted by the many possibilities and agendas that otherwise divert you."[42]

Your vision is the ideal future state, where you are using your strengths and competencies to realize your aspirations. Your ability to recite your vision in a way that captures your yearnings and inspires you to act is truly a competency that, when developed, can help you to achieve your goals more quickly, easily, and with more enjoyment. And your vision will always be unique to you.

For instance, here are two very different personal vision statements:

To serve as a leader, live a balanced life, and apply ethical principles to make a significant difference.
—Denise Morrison, CEO, Campbell's Soup

To have fun in my journey through life and to learn from my mistakes.
—Richard Branson

Companies create collective visions, too. The award for brevity, corporate category, goes to:

To become the world's most loved, most flown, and most profitable airline.
—Southwest Airlines

---

42 Timothy Gallwey, *The Inner Game of Work: Focus, Learning, Pleasure, and Mobility in the Workplace* (New York: Random House, 2001).

Our vision pulls us emotionally and pushes us mentally and physically to the next level. We can bring our vision to life by engaging our strengths to make it so.

Here are examples of how the character strength Perspective and the work strengths Arranger and Futuristic might be useful when Creating Vision.

CREATING VISION WITH YOUR CHARACTER STRENGTHS

Perspective®

Whatever signature strengths you use when forming your personal vision, invite your Perspective to join the exercise. Perspective, the strength, sees what can be best for the task at hand by considering what is relevant to the situation. Not one to be bothered with artificial boundaries or mired in distracting details, Perspective aids the vision creation process by taking into account the short- and long-term achievements it will promote and how to avoid missteps made in the past.

Use your Perspective to extend the dimensions of your vision, bringing it breadth and depth.

If you are a member of the team creating the vision for your organization, invite one with signature Perspective to join you. He can help you see what can and should be included in a new vision that is both desirable and achievable.

CREATING VISION WITH YOUR WORK STRENGTHS

Arranger®

When we look at a written vision statement, we usually see broad categories presented in the order of their importance to the author. Keeping a lot of things in your head and reducing them to the most essential ingredients in the most effective order comes naturally to Arranger.

Denise Morrison doesn't say she wants to expand markets, access resources efficiently, or engage employees. She wants to serve by leading. She uses her Arranger to place leadership on one side of the scale and three other ingredients important to her vision on the other.

Richard Branson makes no mention of a record empire, a transatlantic sailing record, or his airline and space ventures. Whatever he does, he wants it to be fun. I'm betting the list of things that are "fun" for Sir Richard is quite extensive. He uses his Arranger and brevity to summarize and convey the benefit he gets from doing them.

Absent from Southwest's vision are references to passenger comfort, carbon emissions, and fuel efficiency. For what they do, they want to be loved. Their Arranger locates and elevates one state of being, loved, that will best facilitate the future they desire. I'm also betting that Southwest's list of things for which they can be loved is a long one.

Use your Arranger to select the best ingredients for your vision and to present them in the most powerful order. This will propel your intentional action toward what you can and want to be.

Futuristic®

The Futuristic strength, when applied to the Creating Vision competency, can imagine a world in which many things are possible. Use your Futuristic to create a vision that energizes and inspires you and others. To do so, consider the present and add time and excellence. The result: your future.

When Jeff Bezos started Amazon, people thought it was crazy to sell books online. They had no idea that his Futuristic competency was already at work creating a vision of "A to Z" delivery that would bring anything anyone could ever want directly to their door. Now, Amazon Prime is a leading provider of goods and content. This is a powerful example of the Futuristic competency deployed extremely well.

Also use your Futuristic to consider how your other strengths could help you realize your desired state, your vision. Think of some cool ways you could use another of your strengths to accomplish something in the future. Repeat the exercise a few times, with other signature strengths. Look what you have written. You just used your Futuristic to create your own strengths-driven future!

MAKING DECISIONS

The most difficult thing is the decision to act, the rest is merely tenacity.
—Amelia Earhart

After creating a vision, your first step toward realizing it will be to decide how to proceed.

Making Decisions is the competency that, when faced with ambiguous situations and uncertainty, enables you to determine in a timely manner what needs to be done to best achieve your goal.

THINKING CRITICALLY VS. THINKING STRATEGICALLY

This is a good place to address the difference between the two types of thinking that contribute to making solid decisions—Thinking Critically and Thinking Strategically. Here is a compact comparison from Pearson, the learning experts:

> Critical Thinking is a useful mental tool. When thinking critically, we engage the left (analytical) to analyze information and reason in a logical way.

> Strategic Thinking is a mental activity that engages both the left (analytical) and right (creative) sides of our brains. It is the thought process used in order to achieve success. It produces the flow of ideas and associations that can lead to optimal conclusions. It is useful forming a vision, the most appropriate goals to achieve the vision, and a strategic action plan to achieve the goals.

> To think strategically, first think critically.[43]

The competency of Making Decisions is presented in the Thinking Strategically category as a bridge between Creating a Vision and Developing the Plans to realize it.

---

43 Pearson TalentLens©2018, Pearson Education, Inc.

Remember how we consider some strengths to be "free range" because they can be used in one or more sets of strengths? Similarly, some competencies can also be employed to assist in other categories. Making Decisions is one such free-range competency, which you can use in all the other categories of competencies: Navigating Change, Leading People, Driving Results, and Developing Self.

Here are two tools to help you consider the key factors of a problem and make sound and timely decisions: our 5 Step Decision-Making Process and the Eisenhower Matrix.

5 STEP DECISION-MAKING PROCESS

1 *Identify an issue and state why it is important.*
   - What is the potential for gain if you address it?
   - What is the potential for loss if you ignore it?
   What competency-strength combos can you use to define its potential impact?

2 *Gather the information needed to solve the problem.*
   - What facts will be needed?
   What competency-strength combos could you use to investigate the issues?

3 Determine what your options are.
   - What problem-solving approaches should be considered; who will be affected; is time a factor?
   What competency-strength combos will help you compare different approaches?

4   Evaluate the alternatives.
   ▪   What are the benefits and risks associated with
       each course of action?

What competency-strength combos will help you assess
each one?

5   Select the best course of action.
   ▪   Is it one for which you can form feasible plans?

Which competency-strength combos will help you make
your decision?

Use the 5 Steps in concert with the valuable things *you* bring
to the process—your knowledge, your experiences, your bias,
and your intuition. Together, these contribute to something no
outside source can give you—your own good judgement.

Your Judgement + the 5 Steps = Good Decisions

Trust in others is one thing, trust in ourselves is another. When
you combine these three ingredients in your decision-making
processes, you will have earned the right to trust yourself and the
decisions you make.

THE EISENHOWER MATRIX

There are several ways to make decisions well, and many ways
to make decisions badly. We often look to historical figures who
were able to make decisions in key moments and study how
they made them when the stakes were high and the choices felt
limited.

Dwight D. Eisenhower served as the Allied Forces Supreme Commander during WWII, as NATO's first Supreme Commander after the war, and as the 34th president of the United States from 1953 until 1961. This latter period is the time referred to as the Cold War, when the nuclear arms race between Russia and the United States was marked by the mutually assured destruction of both countries if either side launched a nuclear attack. This was the pervasive theme of life in the middle of the last century.

Can you imagine the pressure on Eisenhower to make so many important decisions in rapid succession for so many years? Real life-and-death decisions. Thousands of them. Without the benefit of computers. With millions of people depending on him, how did he do it? One of the answers lay in his view that

What is important is seldom urgent,
and what is urgent is seldom important.

When he had a choice, he spent his time thinking about and doing what he regarded as important but not urgent.

Here is Ike's simple decision-making model.

THE EISENHOWER MATRIX

	URGENT	NOT URGENT
IMPORTANT	**Q1** **DO** *it now* - Emergencies - Deadlines - Demands from above	**Q2** **SCHEDULE** *a time to do it.* - Planning & Learning - Relationships & Family - Exercise & Rest
NOT IMPORTANT	**Q3** **DELEGATE** *it to someone else* - Unnecessary meetings - Doesn't achieve your goal - Technical issues	**Q4** **ELIMINATE** *Stop doing this* - Voluntary distractions - Busy work - Gossip & Worry

Ike's decision-making model served him well in times of crisis. In making the decision to focus on the *Important but Not Urgent* tasks first, he pulled our country through a time of uncertainty and anxiety.

We don't have to have the same strengths as Eisenhower did in order to increase our Making Decisions competency, but we can use his model to identify which undertakings will be worthy of our strengths and competencies. Here are examples of how the character strengths Judgement and Prudence and the work strengths Analytical, Ideation, Achiever, and Context might be used when Making Decisions.

MAKING DECISIONS WITH YOUR CHARACTER STRENGTHS

Judgement®
(abbr. for Judgement/Critical Thinking®)
Judgement, the strength that weighs all the evidence before drawing a conclusion, is the linchpin of solid decisions. How stable can a decision be without the benefit of good Judgement?

No matter how many ideas are on the table, Judgement can use his objectivity to separate the good ones from the bad ones. Before doing so, he will consider each ingredient carefully and from different perspectives.

To improve your Judgement, seek the opinions of others you respect on topics that matter to you. Religion and politics excepted; most people have nuanced views on most issues. Whether their views differ a little or a lot from yours, they may inform how you consider an issue. As you do so, you will strengthen your Judgement.

Use your Judgement to examine other alternatives. Select the best ones and you will make solid decisions.

Prudence®
One with Prudence is careful about her choices and doesn't make decisions that include taking undue risk.

If you or your team feel as if you are rushing to judgement on an issue, ask for the perspective of one with Prudence among her signature strengths. She can help you slow down and reflect more deeply about each element you are considering before making your decision. This pause she brings to the process will help you make a sounder decision.

Use your Prudence to reduce distractions and filter out all the unusable suggestions that we Act Now! on things. With Prudence, you can remain focused on making decisions that will best serve you and others in the future.

MAKING DECISIONS WITH YOUR WORK STRENGTHS

Analytical®
Analytical is an objective problem solver and makes decisions based on the evidence. This quality makes Analytical a desirable addition to any decision-making process.

Think back to a good brainstorming session you attended. When the gray matter gets moving and the blood gets flowing, emotions sometimes run high, right? That's a good thing, except when it isn't. Enter Analytical, to help us refocus on the goal of the session.

Imagine you are in a meeting. Its purpose is to decide which ideas will be included and which will be excluded in an action plan to be drafted. You are leading the discussion and whiteboarding the ideas as they are presented. It's going pretty well. Some good ideas are put forth, then some not-so-good ideas come up, which encourage a couple of crazy ideas to float into the room, leading the conversation to the edge of chaos. What now? Analytical to the rescue, "Hmm…that's an interesting idea. How, exactly, would it work?" 'Nuff said. Depending on the response, the crazy idea gets better—people start slowly nodding in agreement —or it self-destructs somewhere in the middle of the explanation as others raise their eyebrows and look at the table.

Now you've identified the options and addressed issues as they surfaced. The time has come to make decisions. Analytical sits quietly, listening. The to-do list is up on the left, the Eisenhower Matrix on the right. The first item is a definite Q1: DO. The next to-do generates some discussion. There is scattered support for taking it on as a project. Analytical speaks up, "Isn't Taylor in Department X really good at this sort of thing?" Analytical just found a demand-supply match. Off to Q3: DELEGATE it goes. Precious capacity in Q2: SCHEDULE has been saved for more important things.

The last item on the to-do list has supporters in every camp. Whatever the quadrant, someone favors it there. Time passes. Analytical says, "Um, how does this relate to our mission statement?" Oh, it doesn't. To Q4: ELIMINATE and be done with you. Meeting adjourned.

Ideation®

Do any two Strategic Thinking strengths have less in common than Ideation and Analytical? Probably not, but Ideation can also be a valuable one for our Making Decisions competency.

Ideation is the one with the lightbulb over his head. When we want new ideas, we need Ideation to get things going. Connect the dots in new ways.

Back to our planning meeting. We're stuck. With Ideation, not for long. Sooner or later, usually sooner, Ideation will provide a "What if?" to get us going again. As Ideation keeps producing new approaches—he can't help it—we begin to see things in new ways. As we consider them more deeply, Ideation participates but does not feel the need to lead. He's waiting for the next opening that needs a new point of view.

Ideation is great at brainstorming concepts that can lead to better decisions. Back to the session with the to-do list up on the left and the Eisenhower Matrix on the right. You are going down the list—Q1 this, Q3 that, etc. The next item looks like a definite Q4—fuggetaboutit. Until Ideation says, "What if we used this to get Project Y back on the rails?"

What?...How?...Ohh...Great idea, Ideation!

Suggestion: A few nights before a session where you will be Thinking Strategically, take Analytical and Ideation out for drinks. Then leave. As the label on fireworks says, light fuse and run. Let them get to know each other. They will discover all kinds of fascinating things about each other. And you will enjoy their interplay and the contributions they will bring to the decision-making process.

DEVELOPING PLANS

A goal without a plan is just a wish.
—Antoine de Saint-Exupéry

Planning is the process of identifying the best path to reach the most desirable destination. Planning helps you set goals and prepares you to make wise use of your resources to achieve the intended results within a specified timeframe.

Award for Best Definition of Planning goes to Alan Lakein: "Planning is bringing the future into the present so that you can do something about it now." How good is that? It's so good that Amazon sells a laser-cut 8x10 wooden plaque of it. A must-have for you planners.

By Developing Plans, we mean Developing *Achievable* Plans.

Almost anyone can develop a plan.

The difference between a plan and an achievable plan?

An achievable plan is one that embraces the use of signature strengths and the appropriate competencies to produce a desired result. Applying your competency-strength combos to realize a plan greatly improves the odds that you will achieve the best possible outcome.

While we're handing out awards, here's the winning entry for Best Reason Why Planning Is Important:

If you fail to plan, you are planning to fail.
—Benjamin Franklin

There are all kinds of plans you can make: event plans, career plans, marketing plans, succession plans, and plans for the weekend.

Within an organization, Developing Plans competently and strategically is key to moving everyone forward. A well-conceived plan serves as the beacon that will guide leaders, teams, and individuals in their thoughts and actions.

Developing plans, "bringing the future into the present so you can do something about it now," isn't a perfect process. No matter how many plans we create, the future will remain mysterious. What to do when the vision is solid but the big plan to realize it isn't working? Step back a bit to get some perspective. Are the connections between the plan's ingredients solid? If some of them are eroding, can they be repaired? If not, some of the plan's ingredients may need to be reconsidered. Worry not. Take a time-out and pivot—keep your vision but update the plan.

A pivot is a change in strategy without a change in vision.
—Eric Ries, *The Lean Startup*

When planning, start by considering which new competency-strength combos will be best suited to help you reach the goals and you'll be on your way again.

Because your plans are living documents, you will want to keep them out in the open. Schedule a few minutes every other week to review your most important plans. In team meetings, preempt a "Why are we here, again?" mood by referring to the plan at the beginning of the session. This will prepare the attendees to participate in the meeting in the context of the plan.

Here are examples of how the character strength Creativity and the work strengths Input and Strategic might make contributions when you are Developing Plans.

DEVELOPING PLANS WITH YOUR CHARACTER STRENGTHS

Creativity®

Developing Plans is all about finding new ways to do existing things or new ways to do new things. That's one valuable thing someone with a signature strength of Creativity does—he finds new ways to do things that will be useful in developing the most workable plans.

Creativity works at every level. Use your Creativity from the bottom up—to help you find new practical solutions to everyday problems—and from the top down—to help you think differently about the best way to approach big issues.

When you or your team are developing plans and find yourselves a bit stuck, ask one with signature Creativity for his ideas. They may help you address your predicaments with new ways to consider them. As you do so, you will begin to break up the logjam and get on with creating a workable plan.

DEVELOPING PLANS WITH YOUR WORK STRENGTHS

Input®

Inquisitive by nature, Input always wants to know more. Any planning project is better with Input and the library of knowledge he brings.

When the planning team wants to know if a similar issue has been previously addressed, Input may already have something on it. If he doesn't, he is likely the one to know where to find it.

Throughout any planning process, Input is there with the good questions and the information that will lead to better decisions.

Input on a planning team is like having your own private research department!

Strategic®

Strategic sees the big picture.

During a planning process, Strategic can envision the most efficient way to use what we've got to get where we want to go. Few other strengths are as good as Strategic *before* the planning begins, helping the team consider what to include and what to exclude in the plan.

As Strategic encourages discussion on the most important issues, it aids the efficiency of the process. When you want to produce the best possible plan in the least amount of time, Strategic is a good one to have on the team.

Strategic can aid the stability and durability of the planning team by ensuring that strengths from each set will be represented— Thinking Thoroughly, Interacting with Others, Performing with Excellence, and Aligning to Your Values.

For a strategic planning team, maybe the work strengths Futuristic, Strategic, Empathy, Analytical, and Communicating?

For the recruitment committee, perhaps the work strengths Woo, Developer, Positivity, Arranger, and Includer?

For the marketing team, how about the work strengths Adaptability, Ideation, Activator, and Connectedness?

And so on.

Strategic is a natural at this. Don't have Strategic as one of your signature strengths? I'll bet you have a few other strengths you can use to develop your plans.

CHAPTER 8

Navigating Change

Making Transitions

When you're finished changing, you're finished.
—Benjamin Franklin

TOLERATING RISK
NEGOTIATING
COMMUNICATING CLEARLY

Change is the process of becoming different, making the transition from the present to the future. Change can be driven by you or by others. Your participation in change driven by others may be voluntary or involuntary. The change you experience may be gradual or sudden; partial or radical; positive, negative, or neutral. With the Level Up Method, you can navigate whatever types of change you and others bring into your life.

Think of the change process as

Present State→Transition State→Future State

Change is born and educated in the present state, lives in the transition state, and retires in the future state.

There will be change.

Living with a vulnerable present and an uncertain future
is going to be a permanent condition.
—Peter Block[44]

Your Navigating Change competencies will help you bring intentionality to the process of transitioning from the present to the future. With these competencies, you will use your strengths to understand and tolerate the risks, resolve issues along the way, and communicate deeply to ensure everyone is clear on their roles in the process.

Perhaps the best reason to change intentionally:

If you do not change direction, you may end up where you are
heading.
—Lao Tzu, 450 BC

Did Lao Tzu just make the first reference to what's called the Gap?

Next best reason to change intentionally:

If you don't like change, you're going to like irrelevance a lot less.
—Tom Feltenstein

Myth in need of busting: Change is bad. Change is not bad, change is…life. Imagine an unchanging you, frozen in time, motionless. You don't want that, do you? Well, maybe a week flatlining on the beach after a particularly grueling six months might be a nice…what? Yep, change.

44 Peter Block, Flawless Consulting (Hoboken, NJ: Wiley, 2011).

To help us ready our strengths to support our Navigating Change competencies, let's examine the nature of change and how it affects us.

WHAT CAUSES CHANGE?

Change, as we experience it, is usually driven by a mixture of external and internal factors.

A few external causes of change

Money
What money wants money will get.

Speed
Money *loves* speed. Demanders everywhere will pay their suppliers more for speed in goods or services. Who doesn't want their cars, data, and home deliveries to be fast?

AI and the Fourth Industrial Revolution
Money is licking its chops over artificial intelligence and Industry 4.0. The push for data to be faster, smarter, and more conversant with other data has moved from the industrial, agricultural, and service sectors and now has our personal lives in its sights—our cars, our homes, our bodies, our relationships. "Alexa, what time will my wife be home?" Yes, AI accelerates change. But it is up to us to navigate and guide the change. Best slogan of an AI company, this from SAS, the multinational analytics software firm:

Believe in Humans*

* I would add "and their strengths."

Globalization
Driven by technology, transportation, and cooperation, globalization moves capital, information, goods, and jobs to where they will be most useful. To navigate change well, those who lead globalization efforts and those who are affected by them need all the Tolerating Risk, Negotiating, and Communicating competencies they can get their hands on. Poster child for globalization: your cellphone, made and used all over the world and now more powerful than IBM's mighty Deep Blue supercomputer of 1997.

Your Environment
When things around you change, you change.

Organizational Transformation
The word "transformation" sends shivers up my spine. *Harvard Business Review* has found that 70 percent of all organizational transformation efforts fail. That doesn't mean they're not a good thing. Or does it?

Matrix Management
Those of you in these organizations, sitting on multiple teams with multiple leaders, live in a world of constant change. Our hearts go out to you.

Mergers and De-mergers
In "an environment that is everchanging and politically charged," Bain has found that over 50 percent of mergers fail to deliver the results intended. Many studies put the failure rates at 70 to 90 percent.

Think mergers are rough? Their nasty cousins, de-mergers, politesse for balkanization, are the breaking-up of an organization into components to be sold or liquidated. This is change most challenging for those in the units that become untethered from the mother ship.

New Role
Gallup has found that 60 percent of executives in a new role fail in their first 18 months. At the senior levels, all your peers and direct reports have been #1 somewhere. And every one of them who comes through your door has an agenda.

The internal drivers of change

Approach
You want more of something or someone. Money, friends, shiny things, knowledge, and success come to mind. Leading consequence of #1 New Year's resolution in the approach category: gym memberships.

Avoidance
Any *bête noire*—something or someone you want less of. Debt, illness, and anything or anyone that annoys you lead this category. Leading consequence of #1 New Year's resolution in the avoidance category: diet books.

You were expecting a longer list of internal factors? So was I.

On gym memberships and diet books:
Almost any strength can get you into an exciting new self-improvement change initiative. To stick with it, consider how

you might use your character strengths Perseverance or Self-Regulation, or your work strengths Achiever or Discipline.

INTERNAL OBSTACLES TO CHANGE

Whatever you are not changing, you are choosing.
—Laurie Buchanan

What keeps us from navigating the changes deserving of our attention? J. Stewart Black, leader in the study of change, cites:

Three Barriers to Change[45]

1   Failure to See
2   Failure to Move
3   Failure to Finish

What better to help us avoid these pitfalls than our strengths? How about:

Barrier	Character Strength	Work Strength
1 Failure to See	Perspective	Futuristic
2 Failure to Move	Bravery	Activator
3 Failure to Finish	Perseverance	Achiever

---

45 J. Stewart Black, *It Starts with One: Changing Individuals Changes Organizations* (Hoboken, NJ: Pearson Publishing, 2013).

What are the Types of Change?

Most changes are one of two primary types:

Proactive Change	Anticipating the need for change and getting out in front of it. Inverted yield curves and rising tides may be trying to tell us something.
Reactive Change	Responding to signs that changes are needed. Most lie somewhere between the CHANGE ENGINE OIL light on your dash and the stock market crash of 2008 or the pandemic of 2020.

Windows of opportunity open and close. How can you position yourself to be near them when they open so you can participate in the first type of change? When gold nuggets were first found in a California river, which was the better choice: A. to be one of the 300,000 miners; B. to sell them pickaxes, as Sam Brannan did; or C. to make durable trousers for the miners, as Levi Strauss did? Answer: not A.

WHAT ARE THE STAGES OF CHANGE?

The Four Stages of Change[46]

Stage 1	Do the right thing and do it well
Stage 2	Discover the right thing is now the wrong thing
Stage 3	Do the new right thing, but poorly at first
Stage 4	Eventually do the new right thing well

Your competency-strength combos through the four stages:

Stage 1	Current competency-strength combos working fine
Stage 2	Time to rethink your competency-strength combos
Stage 3	Try some new competency-strength combos
Stage 4	Discover the best competency-strength combos to use going forward

WHAT ARE THE CHARACTERISTICS OF CHANGE?

The four types of challenges presented by change are captured in the acronym VUCA.

Volatile	Rapid, sudden change	Earthquake

---

46 J. Stewart Black and Hal B. Gregersen, *Leading Strategic Change: Breaking Through the Brain Barrier* (London: Pearson Education, 2003).

Uncertain	Unclear information and outcomes	Clear air turbulence
Complex	Multiple variables and unknowns	Merger
Ambiguous	Lack of clarity about the meaning of events	Traffic jam

Each VUCA challenge requires its own response. All evade predictability and clear cause-and-effect frameworks. Each Navigating Change competency—Tolerating Risk, Negotiating, and Communicating Clearly—will give you an opportunity to use different strengths to reduce the VUCA in your life.

Examples of strengths you might use to navigate different challenges presented during change:

VUCA	Character Strength	Work Strength	to—
Volatility	**Self-Regulation**	**Self-Assurance**	Promote stability
Uncertainty	**Perspective**	**Analytical**	Reduce un-predictability

| Complexity | Judgement | Arranger | Diminish the # of choices |
| Ambiguity | Creativity | Ideation | Add clarity |

WHAT ROLE SHOULD I PLAY IN CHANGE?

If you choose to navigate change, do you want to be a

Change Agent	and	Promote Change, a
Change Leader	and	Lead Change,
	or a	
Change Manager	and	Manage Change?

It's your choice, depending on how you are wired. There is no right answer. Just know that your default setting may be one role, and what is needed right now might be another. Whichever role you choose, there are no strengths better suited to playing it than your signature ones. Being aware of your role and the strengths you will use is valuable preparation for any change.

Are you ready to negotiate some changes in your own life? Using your competency-strength combos will help you to be more capable and confident. In times of change, you will have an inner excitement as you face new challenges, and an outer calmness that will inspire and motivate others.

During periods of change, every one of your competencies can be helpful at one time or another. We have selected three Navigating Change competencies you will want to place in the top tray of your competency toolbox when, despite all your expert planning, life becomes uncertain. For each of these—Tolerating Risk, Negotiating, and Communicating Clearly—here are a few observations on what it is, why it's important, what it looks like in action, and how to use your strengths to improve it.

TOLERATING RISK

> *What's dangerous is to not evolve.*
> —Jeff Bezos

Every player in every sport has a ready stance. Picture tennis player Roger Federer just before the ball is served to him, light on his feet and ready to spring in any direction.

He's prepared to take the risk that comes with the opportunity to perform.

In times of change, Tolerating Risk is your ready position. Use it to stay light on *your* feet.

Why is tolerating risk valuable to high achievers? Because understanding risks and choosing which ones to take can put you on the path to dramatically better your position in life. Times of change often present wonderful opportunities to improve one's situation. Can you bear another sports metaphor? Think of making personal progress as would a surfer. His ability to increase his velocity greatly improves when he catches a wave. Very few of us are surfers, but all of us can catch waves of change in our lives.

The first step in Tolerating Risk is understanding risk. When you know the potential for gain or loss, how often it may occur, and what impact it might have, you can begin to make decisions about what to do with it. And you will have your first clues about which competency-strength combos to use when you deal with the risk in your way.

The way we approach change, and the risks that come with it, is with a blend of our personal level of risk tolerance and the potential impact the change will have on us. Some of us are natural risk takers, big wave surfers; some of us are risk averse, happy paddling around in the bay on a foam board; most of us are somewhere in the middle, skewing one direction or the other depending on the circumstances and who's watching.

Did you notice that our competency is Tolerating Risk, not Conquering Risk? Conquering Risk would make a fine competency for the Roman god who slays risk. But we are not gods. As humans, our best approach is to try to understand the change around us, to be watchful for opportunities it brings, to influence it when we can, and to see it through. As such, Tolerating Risk is not a one-size-fits-all competency. Tolerating Risk means staying in our ready position throughout the phases of change. Here are three approaches that will help you boost your ability to tolerate the risks that accompany the changes in your life.

3 WAYS TO IMPROVE YOUR ABILITY TO TOLERATE RISK

1   Stay Flexible
2   Manage Your Expectations
3   Remain Resilient

How to accomplish each one of these? With your strengths! Let's see how.

STAY FLEXIBLE

The easiest way to change something is to change your viewpoint.
—Harry Palmer

Happily, our strengths and competencies are situational. Their appropriateness and effectiveness are related to the context in which we use them.

This feature of competency-strength combos is particularly useful during periods of change.

Consider which of your strengths are most helpful in different situations. Think about how you use or don't use your signature strengths to remain positive and adaptable as the conditions change.

For example, during times of change, the social climate around you may shift. Which strengths become more useful and which strengths become less suitable when the atmosphere switches from

Relaxed	to	Formal
Playful	to	Serious
Boisterous	to	Quiet
Optimistic	to	Wary
Thinking	to	Feeling

Will you use different strengths as the conditions change? Of course.

And as you do so, you just might also create some new opportunities for yourself.

During times of change, try different competency-strength combos. Doing so will give you a sense of optimism, better enabling you to tolerate risk. During WWII, when London was under constant threat of bombing, posters throughout the city encouraged

Keep Calm and Carry On

This message, stated with elegance and grace, was a gentle and comforting suggestion to remain composed during a time of extreme uncertainty.

MANAGE YOUR EXPECTATIONS

I always love to be careful with my expectations
so that life has pleasant surprises for me.
—Sebastian Thrun

During times of uncertainty, expectations are the things considered most likely to happen.

The classic advice to manage the expectations of others is to under-promise and over-deliver. But how to manage our expectations of ourselves?

Assigning ourselves unrealistically high expectations has two predictable results: burnout and speed-related incidents, such as train wrecks.

But we also know that low expectations will not propel us to our highest potential.

A nice approach to improving your Tolerating Risk competency is to manage your expectations to the right level, assigning yourself what Daniel Pink calls "Goldilocks tasks—challenges that are not too hot and not too cold, neither overly difficult nor overly simple."[47]

Let's say you want to get in better shape. Examples of Goldilocks tasks would *not* be "Watch someone else do a pushup" (Wally in *Dilbert* might choose this as his New Year's resolution) or "Prepay for twenty 90-minute intense CrossFit classes." But they might include "Walk around the block every day" or "Get an evaluation from a fitness coach."

REMAIN RESILIENT

It's not that I'm so smart, it's just that I stay with problems longer.
—Albert Einstein

During periods of change, we encounter all sorts of difficulties. Resilience is the capacity to recover from difficulties.

With your Tolerating Risk competency, you will be able to handle the inevitable setbacks that come with even the best-laid plans. Using your strengths to tolerate risk will help you navigate both

---

47 Daniel H. Pink, *Drive*, (New York: Penguin Random House, 2009), 118.

expected and unexpected changes. Causes of expected changes: jet lag from a trip across four time zones, office relocation, wife nine months pregnant. Causes of unexpected changes: you won the lottery, surprise merger announcement, global coronavirus outbreak. Which of your signature strengths could help you remain resilient during and after these events?

When you find yourself in the middle of a change created by others, set your sights on a new, achievable intermediate goal. Give yourself one or two Goldilocks tasks.

Say your department and another are going to be combined. Their cultures couldn't be more different. A Goldilocks task would *not* be to ask that you be named leader of the new entity. A Goldilocks task *would* be to volunteer to serve on the committee that evaluates the feasibility of different approaches to combine the two units.

When faced with changes created by others, consider what competency-strength combos you can use to nudge yourself back on the path to your goal. Any that feel like they can help you get back on track are the right ones to use now. Just be like our friend Einstein and stay with it.

Depending on your perspective, the risks associated with change can be exhilarating or frightening. People who like some frightening with their exhilarating love intense amusement park rides. The rest of us are happy on the carousel. Or watching the carousel.

Wherever you are during change, when the building begins to sway, hold on to your signature strengths to comfort and steady yourself.

This, too, shall pass.

Now let's see how the character strength Bravery and the work strengths Adaptability and Positivity can help us tolerate risk.

TOLERATING RISK WITH YOUR CHARACTER STRENGTHS

Bravery®
Those with Bravery may appear to be fearless. More likely, they consider their vulnerabilities and uncertainties just as the rest of us do. Then they act.

Bravery is the courage to address what is uncertain and deal with it as best you can to keep moving through your life. When you engage your strength of Bravery, it can enable you to tolerate risks and respond to them with productive thoughts and actions.

Award for finest advice of how to use your Bravery goes to Ryan Niemiec and Robert McGrath,[48] "When you are at your best with bravery, you take action based on your convictions of what is right, and you face fears and opposition that arise along the way." Bravo, Bravery!

TOLERATING RISK WITH YOUR WORK STRENGTHS

Adaptability®
A utility player is able to play several different positions. During times of change, Adaptability is our go-to utility player. Adaptability's ability to stay in the present and shift approaches when necessary enables him to play any of the three change roles—agent, leader, or manager—in fluid times.

---

48 Ryan M. Niemiec and Robert E. McGrath, *The Power of Character Strengths* (Cincinnati, OH: Via Institute on Character, 2019).

Adaptability, the change agent, identifies opportunities to be productive and gets the ball rolling by accepting change. When a new, well-thought initiative is presented to the team, he is out in front with support for it. His enthusiasm is infectious, moving some of the undecideds to also get on board.

Adaptability, the change leader, is unruffled by the chaos. His clarity about what needs to be done next is inspirational. The way he accepts new risks and weaves them into the way forward serves as a steadying influence on those around him. His confidence that he is on the right path encourages others to follow.

Think of the preflight briefing message, "In the event of a sudden loss of cabin pressure, put your mask on first before helping others." Thankfully, this happens very rarely. When it does, who do you think is the first to take that action? You guessed it—Adaptability, the change leader, tolerating risk by reacting quickly and decisively during a time of sudden change.

As the game changes, Adaptability, the change manager, stays in it. Always in the ready position, he can perform in a variety of circumstances. Adaptability, the change manager, goes with the flow, dealing with uncertainty by doing what he can with what he has. Adaptability loves tolerating risks. It shows.

Positivity®
Change is hard. If there is one kind of person to avoid especially during times of change, it is the negative person. Notice that negativity is not a strength.

Are you familiar with the story of Chicken Little? Chicken Little throws his farmyard into a panic by proclaiming that "the sky is falling!" Versions of this ancient oral European folktale date back many centuries. Don't let a Chicken Little inject chaos into your farmyard by framing the change you are navigating as the beginning of the end. If he wants to play the victim, let him do so elsewhere.

Positivity, on the other hand, can be your best friend during times of uncertainty.

As an optimist, Positivity neither welcomes nor shuns risk. When risk does present itself, and morphs into change, Positivity stays cheery. She chooses to look on the bright side. If she is nearby, her very presence will help you better Tolerate Risk.

When it comes to managing expectations during times of change, we can all welcome the mindset Positivity brings to the process by asking, "What *can* we do?"

During change, at one time or another, you will experience every emotion. Being down is one of them. When that time comes, don't sink; let Positivity throw you a life ring. A bit of positivity will help you see what is right rather than what is wrong with the situation and give you the resilience you need to get back on track. Positivity, like the coast guard, rescues those who swim toward it. When you feel a bit down, look for Positivity and swim toward it. Works every time.

NEGOTIATING

Negotiating is the process of settling your differences with another person or group. The goal of negotiating is to reach an agreement while avoiding an argument.

During times of change, many things may be in motion at the same time—projects, other people, your surroundings, even the rules. To stay or adjust your intended course during change, when external forces are trying to pull you elsewhere, usually involves a lot of bargaining along the way.

Negotiating is another of our free-range competencies, good in a variety of situations. It is especially valuable to have during times of change.

Each of our competencies presents us opportunities to engage multiple strengths. Expert negotiators use their strengths with intention and precision in a way that will have the most impact during important discussions. There are no do-overs in Negotiating. Tip: Before you enter a Negotiating process, mentally lay out the strengths you may summon, as you would items on a buffet. Which strengths will you call upon when, during the proceedings, you want to: communicate verbally in a clear and effective manner, understand the true meaning of what others are saying, create alliances, solve problems, make decisions, or act composed and confident?

Engage your signature strengths to do these things and you will be a full-stack negotiator!

ZOPA, WIFE OF ZORRO?

When using your Negotiating competency, your first goal is to reach a Zone of Possible Agreement, or ZOPA. Also called the bargaining range, this is the place where potential agreement will benefit both sides more than the alternative options. Outside the zone, no amount of negotiation will yield an agreement.

You're coming from the left; the other side is coming from the right. The place where you overlap? That's the ZOPA.

Use your strengths to move into a zone of possible agreement and broaden what you can consider a win, from a point to a range. Say you want to raise the case for an increase in your compensation commensurate with your recently elevated responsibilities. Which of your strengths will support you as you take the conversation to a desirable zone of possible agreement? Hint: Negotiating offers a great opportunity to demonstrate your value to the other side. And your Constellation of Competencies is one of your most valuable features.

Say you did your best to negotiate but could not find a ZOPA where you could reach agreement. Thankfully, there's an exit ramp; you don't have to back up to where you came from. It, too, has a name: BATNA, the Best Alternative To a Negotiated Agreement.

Use this concept when you are unable to come to terms. Seeking a BATNA can be an opportunity to use different competency-strength combos to achieve your new definition of an acceptable outcome. No matter what happens, you will still be in a better place than where you were when you started. And you'll have a lot of new information you can use going forward.

THE 4 STAGES OF NEGOTIATING

To achieve your best result, use different strengths throughout the process of negotiating. Can you see how these strengths could be helpful during each of the four stages of negotiating?

Stages of Negotiating	Character Strengths	Work Strengths
1 Preparation	Perspective	Strategic
2 Exchanging Information	Love of Learning	Communication
3 Bargaining	Creativity	Maximizer
4 Closing and Commitment	Perseverance	Achiever

Are you feeling better prepared to use your Negotiating competency during times of change? You've got the tools that matter—your strengths, the concepts of ZOPA and BATNA, and the roadmap of the stages of negotiating. Use these to fortify your position while the other side is doing whatever it is that they do before you meet somewhere in the middle.

Now let's see how the character strength Perseverance and the work strengths Communication and Self-Assurance might come in handy when we are Negotiating.

NEGOTIATING WITH YOUR CHARACTER STRENGTHS

Perseverance®

Let's get this out there first: negotiating can be difficult. That does not mean it cannot be an enjoyable and informative process on the way to producing results. Most oft-cited reasons why negotiating is difficult include the demands on the participants to be persistent, overcome obstacles, and finish what they started. Know who can be persistent, overcome obstacles, and finish what they start? Someone with Perseverance!

When negotiating, Perseverance sticks with it. This may come more naturally to him than it does to the rest of us, but he still has to work at it. He prepares by organizing himself so that he will be able to remain in the negotiations until they are finished. If you or your team are getting ready to negotiate with one or more parties, invite one with signature Perseverance to join you. His dependability will inspire you to stay the course as you encounter difficulties along the way.

Some days we just don't feel like going on. Perfectly natural. There was this funny cartoon in the *New Yorker*: Executive guy behind a desk in a big office is addressing whomever is outside his office, "I've cleaned off my desk and I'm going home!" On the floor is everything that was on his desk—computer, coffee cup, phone, picture frames, and papers everywhere. Whatever Perseverance he had was not working for him on this day. When you are negotiating, keep your Perseverance handy. Then you can draw upon it when you need a little more strength to keep going.

NEGOTIATING WITH YOUR WORK STRENGTHS

Communication®

Communication, a conspicuous strength, right? Yes, and Communication can also help you amplify your other strengths.

Every stage of Negotiating, from preparation to commitment, benefits from communicating precisely. When negotiating, bring in Communication early and often to convey the desired message.

Use Communication at the front end to gain clarity during preparation. Use it at the back end to confirm the agreement at the closing and commitment stage. Communication is a good one to go to for extra points during this phase. She can use her way with words to pleasantly offer that a covered point isn't in the summary—one that benefits your side—or ask why something that did happen is referred to one way and not the other. Very hard to do these things without Communication by your side

Self-Assurance®

A valuable asset to have during any negotiating process is confidence. Without it, the other side, sensing weakness, may pounce. With Self-Assurance, you don't have to be aggressive or even assertive. Self-Assurance lets everyone know that you are comfortable in a negotiating role, will address issues as they appear, will represent the interests of your side, and will see the negotiations through to an acceptable result.

The other side, sensing Self-Assurance's comfort with risk, will be less inclined to try tactics to destabilize you.

You've heard of marathon overnight negotiating sessions? Often, they involve political or labor issues. The bedraggled participants emerge the next morning, blinking in the sunlight as they try to respond to a barrage of staccato inquiries by a waiting press. What kept them from giving up, going home, and trying it another day?

To stick with it, each side probably benefited from a member who could engage their Self-Assurance strength to get them and their team members through the night. His courage and sense of certainty about the potential for a beneficial outcome encouraged his teammates to stay with it.

You know that change is hard. Negotiating during change can be really hard. Having Self-Assurance and this "We can do this!" attitude can help keep the mood buoyant when the details of complex negotiations are trying to pull you down.

COMMUNICATING CLEARLY

You can't manage a secret.
—Alan Mulally, former CEO, Ford Motor Co

Communicating, the act of transferring information, can be achieved by speaking, writing, or through body language.

Another of our free-range competencies, Communicating Clearly is highly useful at enhancing many of our other competencies. It is introduced under Navigating Change because communicating openly, honestly, accurately, and deeply is crucial to achieving the best result during times of change.

THE 5 ELEMENTS OF EFFECTIVE COMMUNICATION

The five basic ingredients of any efficient communication:

1	Who	The sender transmits
2	What	the message at precisely the right
3	When	time
4	How	in a manner that will be clear to
5	Whom	the receiver
		and accomplishes his intended purpose.

Here are a few examples of how your character and work strengths can be used when you are the who—the sender—or the whom—the receiver—during communications about change.

When sending a message, engage your–

Character Strength	*Work Strength*	*to convey–*
Perspective	Connectedness	What is happening now is just part of life
Prudence	Deliberative	We're being very careful with this change
Zest	Futuristic	Think of what tomorrow might bring
Creativity	Ideation	This is our chance to be creative
Kindness	Includer	This is for all of us
Hope	Positivity	This change is a good change
Honesty	Responsibility	We are going to do what we promised
Bravery	Self-Assurance	This *will* work

When receiving a message, engage your—

Character Strength	Work Strength	to understand—
Judgement	Analytical	What is being communicated
Social Intelligence	Empathy	Where the sender is coming from
Curiosity	Input	What new concepts are being introduced
Love of Learning	Learner	Opportunities for personal growth
Zest	Positivity	The beneficial aspects of the change

THE 5 STAGES OF COMMUNICATING CHANGE

People don't resist change. They resist being changed.
—Peter Senge

Whether you are announcing a merger to your international organization or telling your spouse that your mother is coming to stay for two weeks, the stages of communicating change will be the same:

1 Explain what led to the change.
2 Describe the actions we need to take.
3 Enthuse over the benefits of the change.
4 Provide updates as they become available.
5 Manage the drama.

At each stage, there will be opportunities for you to engage different strengths to achieve the best possible result. Which of your strengths will be useful at each of the stages?

Charles Darwin's investigations led him to understand the organisms that adapt to their environment are the ones most likely to survive. Also true in society. In an organizational setting, a big part of adapting to change and successfully navigating it is sending communications with clarity and receiving them with comprehension at each of the five stages.

If we skip over communicating at any stage, it will be difficult or impossible in the stages that follow. And communicating at each stage is not a one and done affair. Are you familiar with The Rule of 7? The Rule of 7 states that people need to hear something seven times before they understand and warm to it. What this doesn't mean is to repeatedly send the same messages, like a ship's SOS telegraph. Mix and match different forms of communication to accomplish your objectives throughout the change—group presentations, email updates, team meetings, quality mailings, 1:1 conversations, and handwritten notes.

Get out in front of the change, communicate early and often before it becomes too complex to convey. When it comes to methods and channels you use to communicate change, more is better.

W-I-I-F-M?

The most frequently asked question during change is "W-I-I-F-M?"—*What's in it for me?*

If there is a message people *want* to hear seven times, it is the answer to this question.

Gallup has found that, upon being introduced to a prospective change, the typical distribution of responses falls into four segments:[49]

10%	Champions	Eagerly embrace and lead the change
10%	Helpers	Will follow the Champions, encouraging change
60%	Bystanders	Neutral, could go either way
20%	Resisters	If given the chance, will disrupt the change

Each segment will benefit from a tailored communication of the change at each stage:

- Different strengths will support
- Different approaches to communicating with
- Different segments during
- Different stages.

---

49 Copyright 2018 Gallup, Inc.

That's a lot to consider. Too much, really. It will be enough if you are generally aware of the stages of communicating and how others may respond.

YOUR ROLE IN NAVIGATING AND COMMUNICATING CHANGE

A good time to select the role you wish to play is when you sense a forthcoming change is probable. Hint: Pick the role that makes the most effective and pleasurable use of your signature strengths. Do you wish to play the role of change agent, change leader, or change manager?

If you are a–	*you–*
Change Agent	Talk the talk
Change Leader	Talk the talk and walk the talk
Change Manager	Walk the walk

Change Agents get the change going and let others know they enthusiastically support it. If the change makes sense to them, they will be the early adopters and some of its most fervent supporters. Change Agents often work their magic with the help of their character strengths Hope and Zest, and with their work strengths Activator and Futuristic.

Change Leaders see the landscape from above. They take it upon themselves to organize the resources, implement the plan to initiate the change, and keep the major stakeholders engaged along the way. Change Leaders may draw upon their character strengths Bravery and Perspective, and on their work strengths Arranger and Maximizer to bring a change from concept to reality.

Change Agents and Change Leaders can help that big group in the middle, the Bystanders, see the value of changing. Bystanders have a natural "if change is so wonderful, why don't you go first?" attitude. It's not negative, it's just neutral. They don't see the benefit until they observe a few others, the Agents and Leaders, take the initiative. When they begin to understand how participating in the change will yield positive results for them, they are more likely to hop on board.

Change Managers are the boots on the ground, coordinating the work and communicating frequently with those above and below them. Change Managers may look to their character strengths Teamwork and Perseverance and their work strengths Connectedness and Responsibility to help them post results as they manage the change process.

Now let's see how the character strength of Humor and two very different work strengths, Command and Empathy, could be useful when Communicating Clearly during change.

COMMUNICATING CLEARLY WITH YOUR CHARACTER STRENGTHS

Humor®

When Mark Twain said, "Humor is the good-natured side of a truth," he was observing that a bit of levity can make the facts we have to deal with more pleasant. By not being unnecessarily serious, those with the strength of Humor have a positive and gentle outlook on life.

Some things *are* deadly serious. But if we have our health and a sense of security, the extremely serious stuff accounts for a fraction of what is in our lives. For everything else, why not enjoy it as best we can? If you can use your strength of Humor to do so, you will improve the positive emotions and decrease the anxiety of yourself and others around you.

When you find yourself needing to communicate in an unpleasant or boring situation, ask someone with Humor among his signature strengths how he would deal with the same situation. When he shares how he would see and handle being in the circumstance, you may be able to lighten up with how you give and receive information.

COMMUNICATING CLEARLY WITH YOUR WORK STRENGTHS

Command®

Command is a rare bird in the strengths aviary. The rarest, in fact. In times of peace, we often get along with other strengths as proxies for the presence it brings. In times of change, Command's steadying influence can be just what is needed to take us through the storm. His business card says it all:

> Command
> CHANGE LEADER

Command doesn't have to be at the podium in a fancy suit to be effective during times of change. Think of George Washington, how he respected and cared for his soldiers at Valley Forge during the severe winter of 1777–78. Surrounded by the enemy in freezing weather, their clothes in tatters and their bellies empty, the soldiers subsisted, and later thrived, on the comfort they received from his visits, his concern, and his Command. He was out there with them throughout that cold winter, communicating by doing, walking the talk. We owe Washington, his Command, and those soldiers a lot.

When the going gets tough, Command is comfortable taking charge. The way he communicates brings order and control to change and inspires confidence in others. During times of uncertainty, everyone can use a little more of the confidence that Command brings.

Empathy®

When the change coin flips, it comes up either as an opportunity or as a threat. During fluid times, the coin flips often. We already know what to do with opportunities: Seize them.

What about threats? During periods of change, Empathy is a welcome addition. Use Empathy to communicate to all levels at every stage. Empathy is a beautiful strength to have around during organizational changes, such as mergers and transformation initiatives, when people may feel threatened by what is to come:

> *How* information is communicated to employees during a change matters more than *what* information is communicated. A lack of audience empathy when conveying news about an organizational transformation can cause it to fail.[50]

Imagine you, the Change Leader, are at the head of the table, about to conduct a meeting. Its purpose is to introduce your team to the consequences of a forthcoming change, for example how some people's roles may be altered in the coming months.

---

50 Patti Sanchez, "The Secret to Leading Organizational Change is Empathy," *Harvard Business Review*, December 20, 2018.

Suggestion: Seat Empathy directly to your right and give her the encouragement and time to speak. The last thing you want to happen during a pivotal presentation on change is to lose your audience. With Empathy by your side, that won't happen. As you are speaking, she will be listening and observing. Empathy is a very keen observer. When appropriate, Empathy can do what Empathy does best—acknowledge what others are feeling in a way that makes them know they are valued and understood. Every time Empathy does this, she breaks down the beginnings of a little wall that was being erected between you and one of your team members. "DJ, I think you may have a concern about the last topic of discussion. Anything you wish to share with us?" Then wait for it. Don't speak. When DJ answers, you will learn something. And you will be given a precious opportunity to do a better job of communicating during a time of change. Will this make your meetings longer? A little. Will this make them better? A lot.

Empathy—a wonderful strength to include when communicating changes that requires some navigating.

CHAPTER 9

Leading People

Working with Others

The only definition of a leader is someone who has followers.
—Peter Drucker

If you're riding ahead of the herd, take a look back every now and then to make sure it's still there.
—Will Rogers

THE LEADING PEOPLE COMPETENCIES

BUILDING COLLABORATIVE RELATIONSHIPS
INSPIRING OTHERS
DEVELOPING OTHERS
INFLUENCING OTHERS
LEADING TEAMS
MANAGING CONFLICT

Leading People is the ability to help others be successful and feel motivated to achieve common goals. The competencies in this category will provide individuals, teams, and organizations a much-needed and valuable ingredient—momentum.

Without it, progress can come to a halt quickly. Or worse, it can reverse.

An insightful definition of leadership from Donde Plowman, new chancellor of the University of Tennessee:

Leadership is the willingness to act to make things better. Willingness to act is the disruption the world needs.[51]

Your Leading People competencies will enable you to bring value at the front end by attracting high performers, and at the back end by retaining them. The Leading People competencies help to ensure that your talent pool is stable and fresh.

FOLLOWERSHIP

Leaders and followers—you can't have one without the other.

Before we turn our attention to the supply side, leadership, let's look at the demand side, followership. Yes, it's a thing.

Followership is the willingness to work toward achieving common goals.

Both leaders and followers make a lot of decisions as they initiate their actions and take responsibility for them. A major difference between the two is that leaders get to set the goals and followers get to accomplish them, often on teams. Many of our best leaders earned their positions by being great followers.

---

51 Dr. Donde Plowman, Gallup at Work Summit keynote address, June 2019.

Followers are the ones who get the work done. How well they follow is just as important as how well the leaders lead.

Leaders who meet the needs of their followers are doing a great service to both those who depend upon them and to the common goals they all wish to achieve.

Open University tells us, in their Leadership and Followership course, that: "Taking the time to understand the needs of your followers is an important step. Responding to and meeting those needs will allow you to form positive relationships with your team." New Zealand scholars Jackson and Parry[52] explain that followers have several needs and that the leader must attempt to fulfill the need for:

CLARITY[53]
MEANING
SAFETY

A Gallup research team asked over 10,000 followers what the most influential leaders contribute to their lives. The research identified four basic needs of:[54]

TRUST
COMPASSION
STABILITY
HOPE

52 Brad Jackson and Ken Parry, *A Very Short, Fairly Interesting and Reasonably Cheap Book about Studying Leadership, 2nd ed.* (London: SAGE Publications Ltd, 2011).
53 Sandler Training has observed "creating clarity is a leader's most important task."
54 Tom Rath and Barry Conchie, *Strengths Based Leadership* (Washington, DC: Gallup Press, 2008).

Compare these needs with the four discovered by Leigh Branham,[55] to feel:

TRUST
HOPE
SENSE OF WORTH
COMPETENT

As we consider the needs of followers in these three groups, a pattern and a powerful message begin to emerge. Before engaging a Leading People competency, we will want to consider our goals *and* the goals and needs of others. Then we will better able to select the competency-strength combos that will satisfy both.

How good a job are leaders doing at meeting their followers' needs? The Willis Towers Watson Global Workforce Study found that "just under half (47 percent) believe leaders have a sincere interest in employee well-being."[56] Sad.

You've probably heard, "People leave their managers, not their companies."

In Gallup's massive study on 2.5 million manager-led teams in 195 countries, they found that half of all employees have left their job to get away from their manager at some point in their career.[57] A loss of talent for approach reasons—more money, shorter commute, greater opportunity—is one thing. A loss

55 Leigh Branham, *7 Hidden Reasons Employees Leave* (NY: AMACOM, , American Management Association, 2012).
56 Willis Towers Watson, "U.S. Employees Give Senior Leadership Low Marks, Willis Towers Watson Research Reveals," June 22, 2017.
57 Gallup "State of the American Manager: Analytics and Advice for Leaders," 2015.

of talent for an avoidance reason—just to get away from your boss—is quite another.

THE OPPOSITE OF LEADING PEOPLE

Before we get into the positive results that can be achieved from using our strengths when Leading People, let's look at the opposite—losing people—a non-competency if ever there was one.

Losing people is dark, but it is not mysterious. The causes are known.

An insightful look at why followers leave their leaders can be found in Leigh Branham's excellent *The 7 Hidden Reasons Employees Leave*, cited above. For clues about what leaders can do to prevent this, let's see which of a follower's unmet needs might have hastened their voluntary departure and which strengths could have been used to meet their needs.

Below each of the reasons for leaving are a couple suggestions on what needs may have been unmet.

1   Job or workplace not as expected
          Clarity, Safety

2   Mismatch between job and person
          Stability, Competent

3   Too little coaching and feedback
          Compassion, Clarity

4   Too few growth and advancement opportunities
             Hope, Stability

5   Stress from overwork and work-life imbalance
             Stability, Safety

6   Feeling devalued and unrecognized
             Sense of Worth, Compassion

7   Loss of trust and confidence in senior leaders
             Trust, Hope

Which strengths, if they had been demonstrated, could have helped to avoid the problem?

How about these three character strengths
      Love, Kindness, Social Intelligence

and these three work strengths
      Empathy, Communication, Includer

They could have taken the leaders a long way toward meeting the unmet needs of their followers.

An understanding of our followers and their needs is crucial to our ability to lead in ways that are effective and sustainable.

When leaders comprehend the needs of their followers and strive to meet them, both sides are rewarded. Positive effects include a boost to morale and steadier progress toward meeting goals.

BUILDING COLLABORATIVE RELATIONSHIPS

Nobody cares how much you know,
until they know how much you care.
—Theodore Roosevelt

Building Collaborative Relationships is developing positive connections with others and working with them to produce something.

When we have strong collaborative relationships with those around us, our efforts to achieve our goals are more enjoyable and we are more productive.

Of the needs of followers, Trust, Safety, Meaning, Compassion, and Hope are all deeply satisfied by Building Collaborative Relationships.

Building Collaborative Relationships is a big competency, one that takes time to develop. Our competencies are bundles of abilities, knowledge, and skills. A few in the bundle of Building Collaborative Relationships are listening, understanding, communicating, being generous with your time, encouraging others, assisting others, compromising, keeping promises, demonstrating empathy, being open, and being patient.

The thing people most look for in others is a sense of *connection*. Hugs, rubbing noses, and the predecessor to the handshake were early methods used to connect with one another. Next came speech. Then, writing. Later, the telephone and the internet carried the messages that enabled us to build relationships with those not in our physical proximity.

173

Notwithstanding all our brief exchanges on social media, most of our deeper interactions with others still occur during social, career, or recreational activities. They range in scale from the intimate to the immense.

Social	Pleasant Conversation → Mardi Gras
Career	1:1 meeting → All-Hands Town Hall
Recreational	Checkers → Kentucky Derby

A fourth category of deep interaction is collaborating on projects via the internet with a small number of others who are geographically remote. A lot of deep work gets done this way. Early scientists and coauthors exchanged information via horses and boats. We click SEND.

Every interaction with people is a chance to use our strengths to build relationships and collaborate. New opportunities to connect with others often present themselves at intermediate-sized gatherings: dinner parties, team meetings, participating in sports.

Building Collaborative Relationships is one of our free-range competencies. When we use it with our other Leading People competencies, they amplify each other.

Notice how Building Collaborative Relationships and

Inspiring Others	Draws them closer to you.
Developing Others	Gives you an opportunity to help them.
Influencing Others	Aligns others with you.

Leading Teams	Gets everyone in the game.
Managing Conflict	Corrects relationship derailments.

Nice how this works.

ON COLLABORATION

The most productive relationships are collaborative relationships.

Collaboration, working with others on projects that matter to all, is one of the best ways to build durable relationships. The higher the value of the project to each party, the deeper and more successful collaborating on it will be. Collaboration improves everything—better ideas and innovation, improved teamwork, quicker progress toward goals, and work done more effectively.

The most durable benefit of collaborating may be the opportunity it presents to understand and engage each other's complementary strengths. This is synergy of the best kind. A shared goal now sets the stage to work together on other projects in the future.

> The best people to collaborate with: your customers. Always a win-win.

> The next best: anyone with good competencies and different strengths.

> The worst person to collaborate with: someone who is just like you.[58]

---

58 *"When two men always agree, one of them is unnecessary."* —William Wrigley, Jr.

Extend your search for new relationships and collaboration partners to people who are outside your current spheres of influence. Challenge yourself to expand your possibilities. Even when others hold roles at different levels or are in different silos, collaboration—a horizontal form of communication—can be productive with any two people who wish to join forces on something that matters to them.

How *do* we collaborate when our intended others are in different silos, different organizations, different worlds?

First, we know that this can be done. There is a word for it: teaming.

Teaming enables us to capture the advantages of teamwork by collaborating with others who are anywhere. Those of you in matrix management organizations, sitting on different teams with different bosses, know all about this. The rest of us are coming to the party. We're just a bit late.

Amy Edmondson, professor of Leadership and Management at Harvard Business School, is an expert on the benefits of teaming and cross-silo collaboration. She uses a wonderful quotation to demonstrate what it takes to initiate teaming. Like the rest of life, it's mostly a matter of attitude. Here it is:

> *I don't like that man.*
> *I must get to know him better.*
> —Abraham Lincoln

See? You *can* collaborate with "outsiders." Just be like Lincoln and take the initiative.

Initiating cross-silo collaboration will earn you an identity as one who respects others. And it will improve your opportunities to work on the best projects with the best people.

Also, celebrate collaborations between others by acknowledging them and how they contribute to achieving common goals. When you do so as a leader, the collaborators feel respected and everyone else feels inspired to try some of their own collaborating.

Now, a look at how the character strengths of Honesty and Love and the work strengths of Harmony and Relator can contribute to Building Collaborative Relationships.

BUILDING COLLABORATIVE RELATIONSHIPS WITH YOUR CHARACTER STRENGTHS

Honesty®

When parties are sincere in their thoughts and deeds, it lays the foundation upon which deep relationships can be formed. Honesty, the strength that exemplifies truth and sincerity, is one that can help promote building collaborative relationships of the most durable kind.

Those with Honesty among their signature strengths are viewed as the steadier and more authentic among us. Chances are those with a high strength of Honesty also count the value Honesty as one of their core ones. They can be depended on to honor their commitments and not take shortcuts that will compromise what they believe in.

If you wish to build a collaborative relationship with someone, keep your Honesty at the forefront early in the relationship.

Deeply collaborative relationships are based on trust. Trust is based on the perceived honesty of the other party. Use Honesty to display your honesty. If this makes you feel that you are using circular reasoning, worry not: Strengths, characteristics, and values with the same name are different animals.[59]

Love®

Those who exhibit the strength of Love show us they value their close relations with others. You can think of Love the character strength as part of our general love for people and love the emotion as our deepest affectionate feelings for another person. Those with Love among their strengths often use it to contribute to the formation of collaborative relationships that are reciprocal and valued by both parties.

Use your strength of Love to show others you appreciate your collaborative relationships with them. A few ways to do so are by displaying tolerance, empathy, and forgiveness when you work together.

When you find it elusive to engage others with whom you would like to work, ask one with Love among his signature strengths for some ideas. He may help you understand how to initiate relationships by first showing others that you value having them in your life. When they respond with reciprocal gestures, these can be fine bases on which to build the collaborative relationships you desire.

---

59 The cause of the confusion may lie in the number of words that a language can hold. English, the language with the highest word count, comes in at almost 200,000 words. Contrast this with French, at about 60,000 words. Does that mean French is an easier language to learn? Au contraire.

BUILDING COLLABORATIVE RELATIONSHIPS
WITH YOUR WORK STRENGTHS

Harmony®

When building relationships, first impressions matter a lot. Members of the American Society of Pessimists, if there were such a thing, might be intrigued by the contrariness of a new acquaintance. For the rest of us, agreeability gets the relationship ball rolling. No other strength has the capacity for agreeability the way Harmony does.

When you have a potential new relationship in sight, bring your Harmony into the conversation. It works great one-on-one and is even more effective when meeting people in a group. Harmony will add smiles to their faces and increase the appeal of the group or team to others. A gathering of cheery people is more attractive to potential members. Who wants to join those with neutral or worse expressions?

Harmony—use it to seize opportunities to create new relationships for yourself, to improve relationships between others, and to be an aggregable partner.

Relator®

Relator goes deep. And she sees other Relators as people like us. When we meet a person with signature Relator, we may perceive her as a bit distant. Nothing could be further from the truth; Relator is one with whom you can build a deep and lasting relationship.

Relator is the strength that brings Trust, one of our basic needs, to any relationship. Some people create relationships easily, only to see them inexplicably dissolve just as quickly as they were formed. Relators, with their interest in strong mutual partnerships, have a natural ability to find common ground on which deep relationships can be based. Relators are trusted and valued collaboration partners.

INSPIRING OTHERS

Our chief want is someone who will inspire
us to be what we know we could be.
—Ralph Waldo Emerson

If your actions inspire others to dream more, learn more, do more
and become more, you are a leader.
—John Quincy Adams

Inspiring Others is the competency that confidently demonstrates you believe in yourself and others.

As Inspiring Others promotes an atmosphere of positive emotional energy, it begins to satisfy people's need for Hope. Hope is a wonderful foundation on which to build an environment in which there will be support and excitement around working on shared goals.

Seth Godin sums up brilliantly how leaders inspire others:

> Leaders create the conditions where people choose new actions. The choices are voluntary. They're made by people who see a new landscape, new opportunities, and

new options. You can't make people change. But you can create an environment where they choose to. [60]

When you demonstrate your dedication to the shared vision and do your best work no matter the circumstances, others are inspired. Consider Ernest Hemingway's "Courage is grace under pressure." When people see you stay your course under strong headwinds, you inspire them. When the winds blow you backwards for a while, which they will do occasionally, others will be heartened by your perseverance.

Among the needs of followers, Hope, Meaning, and a Sense of Worth are often satisfied by Inspiring Others. When you confidently demonstrate that you believe in yourself and them, people are hopeful that tomorrow will come and that it will be better than today. Most of all, they feel they can be a part of it. People don't ask for guarantees that you will make everything in their lives peachy, but they do want to feel that what they can do will contribute to the voyage.

What are some of the qualities of those you find inspirational? Chances are they include giving others the feeling of being valued, leading by example, and promoting a sense of optimism and purpose. Present-day givers of hope include Oprah, Elon Musk, Richard Branson, Lady Gaga, the Dalai Lama, Jeff Bezos,[61] and Seth Godin. In the last century, Winston Churchill,

60 Seth's Blog, "Leadership," August 16, 2019, https://seths.blog/2019/08/leadership-2/.
61 What inspires Jeff Bezos? This quote by Emerson, tacked on his fridge: "To laugh often and much; to win the respect of intelligent people and the affection of children; to earn the appreciation of honest critics and endure the betrayal of false friends; to appreciate beauty; to find the best in others; to leave the world a bit better, whether by a healthy child, a garden patch, or a redeemed social condition; to know even one life has breathed easier because you have lived. This is to have succeeded."

Jack Kennedy, Martin Luther King, Jr., Nelson Mandela, and Mother Teresa were at the top of the list. Notice how each of these inspirational people acted in ways that demonstrated their care for excellence. They walked the talk and made everyone else feel better about the future. Which of their behaviors could we emulate to be more inspirational to others?

Here are some ways we can use our strengths when Inspiring Others:

Character Strengths	Work Strengths	to inspire others by giving them–
Love	Achiever	encouragement to produce their own accomplishments
Bravery	Activator	encouragement to take initiative
Fairness	Consistency	assurance that they will be treated fairly
Social Intel	Empathy	the feeling that they are understood
Perseverance	Focus	an appreciation that you will see this through
Curiosity	Futuristic	excitement for where we are headed
Love	Includer	the message that they are welcome
Creativity	Ideation	fascination for what is possible
Love	Individualization	a sense that they are appreciated for their uniqueness
Zest	Maximizer	optimism that we are going from good to great
Perspective	Strategic	greater comfort with and confidence in the vision

Inspiring Others is another of our free-range competencies. (When is it *not* a good idea to be inspirational?) Try pairing your Inspiring Others competency with other competencies to enhance their effectiveness. For instance,

Pair Inspiring Others with–   *to–*

Creating Vision

create excitement for what is to come. As you share your word pictures for the future, others will be inspired by the benefits they will receive from being in the picture and working on the goals.

Communicating

send outgoing messages that give hope. Emphasize what is favorable in new information. Communicating positively has a motivating effect on others. People feel grateful for the contact and will be more inclined to join a common effort.

Developing Others

boost the self-confidence of others. Who doesn't love personal attention and encouragement? When we receive them, we feel energized to better ourselves.

Influencing Others

pave the way to being more convincing. Who doesn't prefer to be inspired by people before we are influenced by them?

Leading Teams

be an inspirational leader. Always the best kind.

Because our strengths are situational, they can be adapted to serve us in a wide range of circumstances to achieve a variety of results.

A few scenarios where we can use our strengths to inspire others:

Scenario 1: You, the presenter

Context	You are at a reception, after which you will be the featured speaker.
Strength	Use your Social Intelligence or your Woo to meet and connect with as many people as possible.
Inspiration	Having personally experienced your friendly, open, and understanding demeanor, the audience members will be more receptive to what you have to say.

Scenario 2: You, the team leader

Context	Your team is down 0-14 at halftime.
Strength	Use your Bravery or Competition to give voice to your intention to win the game.
Inspiration	Others will be moved by your willingness to do whatever it takes to beat the other team.

Scenario 3: You, the team member

Context	The committee is stalled by consideration of too many alternatives.
Strength	Use your Leadership or Activator and volunteer to more deeply explore one of the better options and promise to report on it at the group's next meeting.
Inspiration	With your forward movement on one item, committee members will see a loosening of the gridlock and feel motivated to embrace new options.

Is there something about which you would like to be more inspirational? Try creating your own three-part Context-Strength-Inspiration scenario around it.

CULTCHA

When I lived in Southern California, there was this little joke:

Q:	What's the difference between Los Angeles and yogurt?
A:	Yogurt has culture.

Not really true, but still funny, in a Dorothy Parker kind of way.

Organizational culture means "people like us do things like this." It communicates what is important and telegraphs that the organization can be depended upon to uphold its customs at all levels.

The biggest hidden benefit of inspirational leaders may be the positive effect they have on shaping and supporting the organization's culture.

Intentionally creating a culture can be a huge project, one with *a lot* of constantly moving parts that have a hard time staying where they are placed. Or, you can adopt a strengths-based approach and enjoy the benefits that come with it.

TO BUILD A STRENGTHS-BASED CULTURE,

Understand	the strengths of others
Respect	the strengths of others
Appreciate	the strengths of others
Value	the strengths of others

When people feel valued for their unique strengths and are given opportunities and encouragement to use them, they gain a sense of identity and belonging. A strengths-based culture inspires leaders and followers alike.

Valuable benefits of a strengths-based culture include its ease of installation—much is known about strengths—and the strong natural link between the stated culture and the culture-in-action. This baked-in quality assurance is a big deal. A strengths-based culture is what it is. Unlike some other game of "management telephone," it cannot be interpreted differently as it moves through the organization. If we stick with the discoveries of VIA and Gallup from their extensive investigations and don't add too much of our own spin to it, a strengths-based culture will be the same in theory and in practice with every member of every team and at every level in an organization.

A strengths-based culture inspires trust in the leadership team and allows the organization to differentiate itself. Result? Teams have a proven methodology to address common goals and achieve their best results.[62] The organization with a high performance but user-friendly culture retains its top performers and attracts the most desirable candidates. The result is that the customer is better served, which may be the whole point.

TO BUILD A COMPETENCY-STRENGTH-BASED CULTURE,

To your strengths-based culture,

Understand	the strengths of others
Respect	the strengths of others
Appreciate	the strengths of others
Value	the strengths of others

Add:

Help	others use their strengths to improve their competencies

With a competency-strength–based culture, people know how to quickly and efficiently get to work on their goals. If you want your organization to have a high-performance culture, a competency-strength–based culture will do the job.

---

62 "Teams with strengths-based cultures have 32 percent higher performance." Gallup, Inc., 2018.

One last word on changing your organization's culture: Take your time. Slow is better. Get buy-in and unconditional support at the highest levels before doing anything. Introduce the new concepts gradually, so people will have a chance to understand and embrace them. When adoption of the new starts to build among the influencers, you can pick up the pace.

As enthusiasm rises, and it will, keep slightly ahead of the demand with enhancements that make the process interesting, valuable, and enjoyable for everyone.

Here are some ways in which our character strengths Forgiveness, Gratitude, and Humility and our work strengths Connectedness, Includer, and Consistency strengths might be used to inspire others.

INSPIRING OTHERS WITH YOUR CHARACTER STRENGTHS

Forgiveness®
One of the most moving experiences is seeing one in a position of influence give another person a second chance. Watching Forgiveness the strength in action, we are inspired by the character of the forgiver.

Those with the strength of Forgiveness don't feel burdened to carry the memory of every disappointing act of others into the future. They can shake them off and get on with their lives. And they can give those who have let them down another opportunity to show their merit and value. Most of us have behaved badly at one time or another. We have those with Forgiveness to thank that these instances are not the ones that define us. Those who exhibit their Forgiveness of us are an inspiration that we can do better in the future. This type of inspiration, from another's demonstration that they believe in us as much as they do in themselves, can be inspiration of the most lasting kind.

If you find yourself upset by something that someone important to you has done, talk it out with one who has Forgiveness among her signature strengths. She may help you see that the good of the other person far outweighs this most recent transgression and that whatever it is they did can be pardoned.

Gratitude®

Have you ever been inspired by ones who tell you they feel blessed? Me, too. These lucky souls are also telling us something else, that they enjoy going through life with their strength of Gratitude.

Most of us find happy people to be inspiring. Where do they get their happiness? Maybe from this link:

Gratitude→Satisfaction→Happiness

Feeling and acting grateful, we are more satisfied. The more satisfied we are, the happier we are. The happier we are, the happier others are. The happier others are, the more inspired they become. A stretch? Maybe, but my money is on the Gratitude-Inspiration connection. It makes the case that openly expressing our strength of Gratitude can promote inspiration in others.

When you sense someone isn't feeling satisfied with his life, bring your strength of Gratitude into a conversation with him. We all have a bit of "monkey see, monkey do" in us, the natural tendency to mirror the emotions and actions of others. Your expression of Gratitude in your life may trigger him to feel some of his own and, you know where this is going, he may feel inspired by you and your enabling words.

Humility®

When those with the strength Humility demonstrate that they feel we should be recognized before they are, we feel inspired. When the awards for being wonderful are passed out, they prefer to receive theirs last.

Use your strength of Humility to let others know you want to lift them up and celebrate their contributions. They, sensing your healthy self-esteem *and* regard for their place in the grand scheme of things, will feel drawn to and inspired by you.

Many of our strengths contribute to our ability to take charge. Command, Significance, Competition, and Self-Assurance are among them. They are highly useful when getting things done with others. But to stay balanced as a person, we need our pendulum to occasionally swing the other way. Humility can help it do so. When we engage it, we will continue to have all our take charge strengths and will add an ingredient that can help us also be unpretentious. And more inspiring.

INSPIRING OTHERS WITH YOUR WORK STRENGTHS

Connectedness®

Connectedness, the strength, knows that we are all part of something larger than ourselves. The competency of Inspiring Others involves confidently demonstrating that you have faith and trust in yourself and others.

Those with Connectedness have a conviction that things happen for a reason and that everything is somehow part of a bigger picture. When Connectedness lets others know that *they* are also in that picture, it has a calming effect. People feel more certain about their relationships, more optimistic about collaborating, and inspired by Connectedness's assurance that we are all in the same boat.

Using your Connectedness to build and strengthen your relationships helps others feel less vulnerable in the face of unpredictability. Your confidence is inspiring and stimulates others. What better gift to bring into a relationship than a boost to the other person's confidence? Your Connectedness will do that.

Includer®

Includer wants everyone to be on the inside. When you let others know that they are part of your world—your goals, your successes, and your celebrations—they feel a lift. Your interest and support inspire them.

Includer is not seeking homogeneity. Includer is fine with differences in people and perspectives. When others sense this, they feel your acceptance of them. People are encouraged by the sense of safety that inclusion provides. They feel energized and inspired when all are welcome.

Life can be chaotic. Includer dampens a common effect of chaos—the feeling people get that they may suddenly become untethered from their community. Includer says, "No, you're right here with us, just like everyone else." Includer is very good at Inspiring Others during times of uncertainty.

Consistency®

Consistency is keenly aware of the importance of treating all people the same. Consistency, with its innate sense of fairness, has a steadying effect on others, preparing them to be less anxious and more receptive.

When people feel uncertain about their environment, they are about as far from being inspired as they can be. A cause of uncertainty in social groups or professional organizations can be the perception of favoritism. Whether real or imagined, when people feel that others are getting a better deal than they are for no good reason, their morale plummets. It takes with it their ability to be inspired. A temporary approach to Inspiring Others may be whipping them into a lather with overenthusiasm. A more durable approach to Inspiring Others is to act in ways that give them a sense of stability and that they will be treated fairly.

Consistency, with its quiet and deep sense of equality, has a calming effect on others. Consistency helps create an environment where people can focus more on what they are doing and less on how others are being rewarded. The reduction in anxiety they experience brings Hope for the future. People feel more inspired about their prospects.

DEVELOPING OTHERS

The greatest good you can do for another is not just to share your riches but to reveal to him his own.
—Benjamin Disraeli

Leading People, the category of competencies, enables us to make a difference in the lives of others in a variety of ways.

The competency Developing Others involves demonstrating our care for people and our willingness to assist them. As we develop others, we encourage and help them improve so they can make progress toward their goals. When we choose to develop others, we can make a big difference in their lives.

Developing Others deepens the level of engagement and increases retention of those with potential. When you turn your attention to helping others improve, everyone benefits. The recipients of your efforts appreciate the support and the momentum you bring them. Seeing this, others are encouraged by the availability of this path to advancement. As Developing Others promotes talent acceleration, both morale and productivity improve.

The leader also benefits. Those who develop others enjoy the impact it has on reaching common goals and the personal satisfaction it brings them. This thought from Dorie Clark captures it perfectly:

> *Once you've achieved your own goals, the next—profoundly fulfilling—step is to help teach others how to achieve theirs.*[63]

When you focus on assisting those with key responsibilities, you don't have to understand and control everything in your organization. The more others are engaged and take credit for their results, the easier your job. An investment-grade competency, Developing Others can pay dividends for years to come.

Developing Others can have deeply satisfying effect on five of the needs of followers—Compassion, Meaning, Hope, Sense

---

63 Dorie Clark, *Stand Out* (New York: Penguin Random House, 2015).

of Worth, and Feeling Competent. When you develop others, you demonstrate your concern for them and your willingness to help them. When people feel that you *want* them to be the best version of themselves, they sense that you care. Playing an active role in everyone's personal development is neither your goal nor a necessity. Just knowing you believe that all deserve a chance to reach their potential will go a long way to providing people a sense that they are in a place where they can achieve personal growth.

THE T-SHAPED INDIVIDUAL

To help another reach their goals, consider where their potential lies and in which direction you will guide their development, in breadth or in depth.

Have you heard of the concept of the T-shaped individual? A T-shaped person has deep knowledge and skills in a specialty *and* the ability to make connections across different disciplines. The horizontal top of the T symbolizes a breadth of general knowledge and "soft skills." The vertical stem of the T symbolizes depth of thinking and "hard skills." As you might imagine, it is quite a special person who is both a niche specialist *and* a generalist with people skills.

The most intensely vertical person would be a specialist, an expert in one thing:

The extreme version of a horizontal person would be a generalist, with a breadth of knowledge and skills in many areas and no depth in any one of them:

The T-Shaped person is both a generalist and a specialist, capable of many things and possessing a deep knowledge of one or more of them:

When helping others develop, consider the direction in which their contenders can help them improve. If we place the categories of competencies on the T, it might look like this -

LEADING PEOPLE ——————— DEVELOPING SELF

THINKING STRATEGICALLY

NAVIGATING CHANGE

DRIVING RESULTS

Generally:

Leading People and Developing Self are categories of competencies that benefit from horizontal expansion. More is usually better.

Thinking Strategically, Navigating Change, and Driving Results become more focused as they go. For them, deeper is usually better.

BE A SERVANT LEADER, LIKE A SHERPA

When you choose to develop others, you self-define as a servant leader. This is an ancient concept that was given its modern name by Robert Greenleaf in an essay exploring why authoritarian leadership wasn't working.[64] He posited that power wielded from above is inferior to power that is shared. The servant leader puts the needs of others first, helps people develop, and shares power. For a model of this approach, consider the Sherpa. Sherpas, Tibetan climbing guides, prepare the route and guide their expedition party to the top of the mountain. They help those with the greatest capabilities to reach their full potential. Sherpas are excellent servant leader role models for those of us who develop others.

An advantage of the servant leader approach to Developing Others is that, with high achievers, a modest investment can yield significant returns. As you help others get the hang of using their competency-strength combos to work their initiatives, you give them forward motion. High achievers usually respond by adding momentum of their own. A lot. You don't necessarily

---

64 Robert K. Greenleaf, "The Servant as Leader," essay, 1970.

need a detailed framework with mileposts and metrics to help high potentials get better. This isn't managing we're talking about, it's leading. Bright people don't like to be over-instructed in prescriptive programs.

> *Grass doesn't grow faster if you pull on it.*
> —African proverb

Use the Level Up Method to make another's voyage of discovery interesting and productive and you will be working on your own winning strategy—spending your precious time and energy on high-potential projects and high-potential people. Like Sherpas do.

High achievers and high potentials want jobs in which they can develop personally. If your organization wishes to provide opportunities to support personal development, embracing the Level Up Method and our 7 Step framework will do it for you. Win-win: You give your valued team members opportunities to improve themselves and receive the benefits of their increased productivity and engagement.

Developing Others is the "children are our future" of the competencies. Let's see how the character strength of Kindness and two work strengths, Individualization and Maximizer, can help us prepare others for their best futures.

DEVELOPING OTHERS WITH YOUR CHARACTER STRENGTHS

Kindness®
Developing others begins with your decision to assist their improvement and moves quickly to how you express it to them—

as a question, a suggestion, or an offer. What better strength to include in that communication than your Kindness? One who demonstrates Kindness when developing others lets them know he has concern for their well-being and truly wishes them the best.

Expressing your Kindness when developing others gives them a sense of safety and a desire to please you during their process of improvement. This has a motivating effect on them and provides you a nice return on your investment. A world with more kindness in it is a better world. And people who demonstrate Kindness feel better. When you do something for another, don't you get a little lift? That's your complimentary shot of serotonin, the neurotransmitter that gives us the feeling of satisfaction and well-being we get when we are kind to others. But wait, there's more! When you express your Kindness to others, you also receive a dose of endorphins, released when we are generous to others. The effect this has on us is coined "the helper's high."

Do you know some strong-willed people you would like to help take their lives to the next level? Rather than match their demeanor, which might promote a sense of competition, consider coming in from the opposite direction, with your Kindness. Be like Androcles,[65] the escaped slave who pulled the thorn from a mighty lion's paw. In return, the lion licked Androcles's hand like a friendly dog. The emperor, impressed with Androcles's kindness, pardoned and freed him. When approaching those strong-willed people you would like to help develop, consider them as lions in need and yourself as Androcles.

---

65 One of the wonderful fables from Aesop, c. 600 BC

DEVELOPING OTHERS WITH YOUR WORK STRENGTHS

Individualization®

Lucky is the person who has someone with Individualization to guide their development. Individualization, the strength that sees the unique qualities of each person, can dial in to what makes people special and how they might use what they've got to get where they want to go.

Have you ever seen plate spinners at the circus? They try to spin as many plates as they can on top of poles without the plates falling off. The spinner pays keen attention to each plate, darting back and forth to attend to the ones that need some more momentum. Individualization is like that when Developing Others. Intrigued by the unique qualities and requirements of each person, Individualization can give them what they most need when they need it. By the way, the record for the most plates spun simultaneously is 108. It took a lot of Individualization to do that!

Use your Individualization when Developing Others. Let them know that you see their unique characteristics and that you believe in their potential. And give them some of whatever will keep them in motion.

Maximizer®

Maximizer is the good-to-great strength. Maximizer doesn't go anywhere near fixing weaknesses.

Use your Maximizer to bring optimism and a sense of self-worth to others as you help them develop. Your Maximizer sees the potential in them and will set the bar at a height you know they can clear, one that will give them a new personal best.

As you engage your Maximizer when Developing Others, your encouragement will give them a lift and help them reach their potential. With your support, they can resign their Flat Earth Society memberships because, now, there are many new places they can go. Use your Maximizer when Developing Others and enjoy the multiplier effect it will have on the process.

INFLUENCING OTHERS

Leadership is the art of getting someone else to do something that you want because he wants to do it.
—Dwight D. Eisenhower

One big thing high achievers and leaders do to reach their goals is influence others. Influencing Others is the competency to indirectly shift how people think and act. The purpose of influencing the people you lead is to help them improve their chances of producing positive outcomes.

Influence is an important part of leading others. Done right, it helps people understand and embrace the common goals and increases their desire to work toward achieving them.

Influencing Others also benefits the leader. The leader's ability to wield influence is an important qualification to steering an organization effectively. Leaders work with others at all levels—above, across, and below them. The leader's aptitude for persuading others to support the goals is crucial to his success.

Of the needs of followers, Meaning, Hope, Clarity, and Stability are often satisfied by demonstrating the competency of Influencing Others. When people feel you want them on board with the plan that is best for everyone, they gain a sense of confidence in your plan and the organization. In turn, they will be more likely to support your programs and respond favorably to your requests.

Remember the additive nature of our competencies, such that the three preceding Leading People competencies have prepared you to now improve and make use of your *Influencing Others* competency.

> *Building Collaborative Relationships*, you connected others to you. People prefer to be influenced by those they know and trust.

> *Inspiring Others*, you gave them hope. To be influenced, people first need to feel inspired.

> *Developing Others*, you helped them improve their ability to succeed. As people experience your interest in their improvement, they sense compassion and are encouraged to use their new capabilities and knowledge to accomplish something.

When you demonstrate these competencies, you have an energizing effect on others.

Other people can't directly motivate us. We have to do that for ourselves. But others can influence us. There is a powerful adage that describes the relationship between motivation and influence:

Motivation gets you going.
Influence is what makes you go in a particular direction.

Think of the people who are influential in your life. What do they have in common? The first thing that usually comes to mind is that they are confident. Does their confidence come from competence? Probably. Another thing we notice about influencers is they know what they are talking about. They've done their homework. What's more, they can read their audience. They often know a lot about the people who are important to their lives because they took the time to build relationships with them. When influencers demonstrate these attributes, we perceive them as trustworthy.

To be a successful leader, having good ideas or creating change initiatives isn't enough. Getting the work started and continuing requires Influencing Others. It's a big part of the leader's job. Good leaders view their role as a responsibility rather than a privilege. They work hard to earn trust. Building Collaborative Relationships, Inspiring Others, and Developing Others are fine ways to build trust. Leaders and high achievers who do so prepare people to be influenced. And the leader earns the right to influence them.

TO INFLUENCE, USE THE THREE CS

Aiming your influence in the direction of your goals and objectives will help you achieve them. When you have an idea of what you wish to accomplish by Influencing Others, create a roadmap for how you will go about doing so. An easy-to-remember and effective framework for Influencing Others is Connie Dieken's Three Cs of Communication:[66]

66 Connie Dieken, *Talk Less, Say More* (New York: Wiley, 2009).

CONNECT →   CONVEY →   CONVINCE

Know your audience   Be clear   Lead others to act

Simple, straightforward, and useful. Which strengths could you engage to help you influence others? Maybe:

	your character strength	*your work strength*
Connect with	Social Intelligence	Empathy
	Love	Includer
Convey with	Honesty	Communication
	Kindness	Positivity
Convince with	Zest	Futuristic
	Leadership	Maximizer

HOW DO PEOPLE LIKE TO BE INFLUENCED?

As you apply these three steps to influence others, you will use your strengths to communicate in a variety of ways. Any one of several will help you get your point across. Here are a few vehicles that can carry the freight of your message and some strength pairings that will enhance their effectiveness:

Facts
Some people need proof. For them, try using your character strength Perspective or your work strength Strategic to reveal the planning that went into the initiative. Use your character

strength Judgement or your work strength Analytical to examine why it is important and beneficial.

Stories
Who doesn't like to be told a story? Try using your character strength Creativity or your work strength Ideation to tell a tale of what is possible, punctuating it with Positivity and Zest to make it attractive.

Pictures
The leader's vision is often a complex one, much like a lengthy play. To inspire others, it's better not to overshare and challenge attention spans. Instead, take a mental snapshot of a pleasant scene that awaits them. Use your character strength Perspective or your work strength Futuristic to paint a word picture and your character strength Kindness or your work strength Includer to let them know that they are in it.

Emotions
For some, a concept must feel right before they can put their support behind it.

Use your broad bandwidth character strength Social Intelligence and your work strength Empathy to let them know that you understand their concerns. Then draw on your Responsibility to signal that you are dedicated to seeing this through.

TO ENGAGE OTHERS...

...build collaborative relationships with them, inspire them with a strengths-based culture, aid their personal development, and influence them to be part of the solution.

How engaged people feel in their organizations and their work is a big predictor of success. Gallup has found that "the percentage of 'engaged' workers in the US, those who are involved in, enthusiastic about, and committed to their work is about 1/3 of the total workforce" and that "organizations that are the best in engaging their employees achieve earnings-per-share growth that is more than four times that of their competitors."[67]

Further, "these companies educated team leaders on a new way of managing—relying on high development and strengths-based competencies. And they held managers accountable for these competencies."

This is strong support for our case that

> *The influence of leaders and high achievers employing strengths-based competencies leads to exceptional levels of engagement and performance.*

Engaging with others and influencing them play a big part in *all* our relationships—not just down, but up and across. Your Level Up competency of Influencing Others also gives you a way to use your strengths to influence those above you—"managing up" to create alignment with your leaders, and to either side, collaborating with team members and other departments.

You are now ready to employ your Leading People competencies to do what may be the most satisfying activity in an organization—Leading Teams.

---

67 Gallup poll, 2018.

First, let's look at how our character strength Kindness and two of our work strengths Developer and Significance could be used to Influence Others.

INFLUENCING OTHERS WITH YOUR CHARACTER STRENGTHS

Social Intelligence®

The first step in influencing others is gaining their trust. A keen observation of a way we can use our Social Intelligence to gain trust can be found in this excerpt from an article by Brianna Wiest in *Forbes*.[68] She observes that those who demonstrate their Social Intelligence

> consider other people's motivations more than their behaviors. Rather than judge or be perplexed by the actions of others, they always consider why someone is doing what they are. Human behavior is only mysterious until you understand what individuals are inherently motivated by.

We feel that those who understand why we are the way we are "get us." When they do, we perceive them as more deserving of our trust. And we are far more likely to be influenced by those we trust than by those we don't.

For example, say you are having a bad day but must attend an important meeting. The other party, or the team leader, may sense that you are not behaving as yourself because of something that is happening elsewhere in your life. When you know that he sees this and holds you less accountable on this day, your trust

---

68 Brianna Wiest, "13 Things Socially Intelligent Leaders Do Differently," *Forbes*, May 13, 2018.

in his judgement increases. And your trust in him increases. And you are more likely to be influenced by him in the future. All these links…everything is connected. Somehow, right?

INFLUENCING OTHERS WITH YOUR WORK STRENGTHS

Developer®

As you engage your Developer when leading others, you send a message that you see potential in the person. You encourage him to grow in ways that will increase his productivity and enable him to contribute to reaching a shared goal. As you do so, your Developer has an influential effect. When someone does something for us, one of our responses may be to find a way to do something for them. Influencing people to do what *they* want to do is the kind of leadership that Dwight Eisenhower was referring to in the opening quotation of this section.

Engaging your Developer when Influencing Others produces a powerful but subtle competency-strength combo that can achieve a win-win for both the provider and the recipient.

Significance®

Significance, a rare strength, is one we do not often witness. But it is well suited to help us influence others.

Significance, determined to do what it can to make the world a better place, also encourages others to reach for the stars. Because Significance is goal oriented, it avoids unimportant tasks. When it does so, others are influenced to do the same, to focus on the essential and make a difference themselves.

Significance, stimulating to be around and very good at Inspiring Others.

LEADING TEAMS

All of us are smarter than any of us.
—Douglas Merrill

A team is two or more people working together to achieve a common goal. Your team, whether you are the leader or a member, is your tribe. You and the other members of your tribe use your unique abilities to provide forward momentum toward the common goal.

Leading Teams means providing them guidance, direction, and encouragement for the purpose of achieving desired results.

Why is Leading Teams important?

Never doubt that a small group of thoughtful committed citizens can change the world; indeed, it is the only thing that ever has.
—Margaret Mead, cultural anthropologist

When Margaret Mead said this, she was talking about teams— not just any teams, but those whose members were thoughtful and committed. What better goal for us here than to investigate how to help the teams we lead be thoughtful and committed?

The best case for the creation of organizations is to bring people together to work on projects in teams. High-functioning teams improve the flow of information and increase the quality and speed of work. Working on teams gives people a sense of belonging, purpose, and accomplishment.

How important is it to be a member of a team? When we consider that membership on a well-led team is a powerful way to meet followers' needs for Meaning, Safety, Stability, Hope, and a Sense of Worth, we begin to understand why teams are so important. As you act capably and professionally when Leading Teams, you give others confidence that their environment is a stable one and will provide them a sense of worth. People feel their strongest connections in an organization when they are working with other team members on shared goals. Being a member of a team, the basic work unit, provides them an identity. Your leading of the team helps meet the five important needs mentioned above.

Earlier, we raised the question about the existence of "born leaders." Not sure there is such a thing, but there are a great many self-made leaders. Want to be one of them? Here are some tips:

THE 10 THINGS GREAT TEAM LEADERS DO

Great team leaders

 1 Paint an attractive vision and set clear, achievable goals for their team

 2 Encourage every team member to use his or her strengths

 3 Have an individual relationship with each team member

 4 Take an interest in the development of each team member

5 Communicate openly, honestly, and frequently

6 Inspire and influence their team members to make progress on goals

7 Praise all achievements

8 Celebrate all wins

9 Manage the drama

10 Don't take themselves too seriously

Leading a group is one thing. Leading a team is another.

- A gathering of people with different skill levels and interests is a *group*.

- A gathering of people with similar skill levels and a common goal is a *team*.

I'm not sure it is even possible to lead a group. Have you ever been to a public city council or HOA meeting? Members of groups don't naturally play well together because their primary interest is self. Because of this, facilitator might be a better description of the one at the podium before a group.

But members of all kinds of teams can work well with one another—customer service teams, the strategic planning team, ad hoc teams formed to accomplish one specific goal—if the members of each team have similar skill levels and want to achieve something together.

Strong teams, and the bonds their members feel between one another, attract talent.

High performance teams do not want low performers on their teams.

> An individual's weakest link is whatever gets in the way of their best.

> A team's weakest link is the weakest person doing whatever they do best.[69]

Yes, the subject of this section is Leading Teams, not being a member of them. But many great leaders were once great followers. Not a leader yet, but want to prepare yourself to be one? As with any role, rehearsal improves the performance. Just imagine you are a leader and you will quickly begin to think as leaders do, act as leaders do, and communicate as leaders do. Really. Try it, it works. When you see an interesting or challenging situation, think W-W-L-D…What Would a Leader Do? You may be surprised at how interesting this exercise can be.

As you use your competency-strength combos on team goals, you become a more valued member of the team. Each time you do so, you pull yourself up a notch on the team ladder. One day, you'll be at the top. If you've rehearsed for your leadership role, you'll be ready.

Great teams, like great leaders, are made, not born.

Of what are great teams made? These seven components will set up any team to be successful.

---

69 CliftonStrengths Summit, 2018, Gallup, Inc.

THE 7 INGREDIENTS OF GREAT TEAMS

1   *Clear Goals*
    Teams that have a vision and know what is expected of
    them get up to speed more quickly and can maintain
    their progress to the desired destination.

2   *Defined Roles*
    When team members play the parts that best use their
    signature strengths, they will achieve more and will be
    sought-after collaborators with other team members.

3   *Commitment to be a strengths-based team*
    Gallup has found that strengths-based teams are more
    engaged, more productive, and experience lower
    attrition.

> *Good leaders make people's strengths effective
> and their weaknesses irrelevant.*
> —Frances Hesselbein, former CEO,
> Girl Scouts of the USA

When team members intentionally use their strengths
to improve their competencies, they become more
capable of filling their roles and collaborating with
other team members who have complementary
competency-strength combos. This leads to

- fewer false starts
- better task allocation
- less misunderstanding

- fewer player changes
- fewer missed deadlines

It also promotes optimism and enthusiasm that the answers the team seeks can be found within. The result of optimism and enthusiasm? Productivity.

4   *Well-defined path to results*
Team members who are given the map and itinerary of the journey can be more confident and focused. High achievers want to know where they are going. When they do, they will always know where the team is today and understand what they need to do to help the team get to the next waypoint.

5   *Open and honest communication and collaboration*
An appreciation for each other's competencies and strengths sets the stage for open discussions about how each member can use what they've got to help themselves and the team. This promotes productive relationships and improves the team's morale.

6   *Frequent progress reports—for learning, motivation, and course correction*
"Updates as they become available" builds trust in leadership and confidence in the process.

7   *Celebrate wins at every opportunity*
The members of great teams are generous with their praise for the contributions and accomplishments of others. A splendid way to start regularly scheduled

meetings is by celebrating a win. Let the others know of something special that a team member recently did. Congratulate the person and ask him or her what competencies and strengths they think they used. People like to be asked how they pulled something off. And the others enjoy hearing how someone else got something done. Once you have started a few meetings with the celebration of wins, people will find part of themselves looking forward to going to a meeting. Crazy, huh? If they are smiling as they come in the room, you know it's working. Better than donuts! Well, almost.

Also celebrate wins at the end of team meetings. Just before you adjourn, provide an opportunity for others to mention something positive that recently happened in their lives. Do an informal voluntary roundtable, asking if anyone has something to share for the good of the team. Do this and you will close your meetings on a positive note.

These little celebrations of wins can make a nice set of bookends to your team meetings.

Another benefit of providing the 7 Ingredients to your team is the trust it will bring—trust in a well-thought-out and supportive environment that team members can depend on to be there for them in the future.

PEOPLE ARE POINTY; TEAMS SHOULD BE ROUND

We know from Gallup's study of strengths that, to develop as individuals, we must be willing to give up being well rounded and choose to invest in our strengths. But while "individuals should be sharp, a team should be well rounded."[70]

When you encourage the presence of different strengths on your team, people will appreciate and begin to celebrate their differences. Team members will come to understand that it is okay if they are great at some things and not very good at others. They will see that they can rely on other team members and their unique strengths to help get the work done.

As Todd Rose notes in *The End of Average*, "talent is always jagged."[71]

In his first principle of individuality, the jaggedness principle, he notes that "almost every human characteristic that we care about—including talent, intelligence, character, creativity, and so on—is jagged."

The well-rounded team has a broad bandwidth of strengths and competencies. Its members focus on using their unique strengths to improve their competencies rather than spending time trying to fix their weaknesses. This enables them to accomplish together what they could not as individuals.

---

70 Gallup, Inc., 2013.
71 Todd Rose, *The End of Average* (New York: HarperOne, 2016).

AIM FOR DIVERSITY

I recently heard this terrific description of diversity by Janina Kugel, chief human resource officer and operating board member of Siemens AG:[72]

> *Diversity is embracing each other's uniqueness;*
> *where everyone can be whoever he or she is.*

A diversity of strengths is essential for teams. There is a real danger in homogeneous teams that they will reach agreement without careful consideration. Often, the result is groupthink—where differing views and creativity are discouraged.

A strong, diverse team has members with signature strengths in each of the five sets.

This variety and balance of strengths add to the stability and productivity of the team.

There is a lot of talk now about diversity and inclusiveness. The welcoming of different strengths is diversity at its deepest and best—bringing together and celebrating what is *internally* different in people by engaging their unique strengths and perspectives to achieve a common goal.

Everyone's signature strengths bring diversity to a team. Strengths-based teams value each person's special abilities and the contributions they make.

---

72 Janina Kugel, Gallup at Work Summit keynote speech, 2019.

Looking to provide or join an inclusive environment? Create or associate with a strengths-based team!

THE SECOND LAW OF WHAT?

Why, the second law of thermodynamics, of course.[73]

> *There is a natural tendency of any isolated system*
> *to degenerate into a more disordered state.*

Isolated systems are defined as those not taking in energy.

What better way for a team to take in energy than to include a variety of strengths and competencies for the purpose of encouraging collaboration and making new discoveries?

If you can do most of the 10 Things Great Team Leaders Do and provide your team the 7 Ingredients of Great Teams, you will be a great team leader and can still be your pointy self.

Let's see how the character strength Teamwork and two work strengths Competition and Arranger might be used to better lead teams.

LEADING TEAMS WITH YOUR CHARACTER STRENGTHS

Teamwork®

Teamwork, the strength that helps us to be a loyal contributor to our team, is a desirable one for any member of a team. For the

---

73 Do you really want to get into this? Okay. You may have heard of the principle that energy can be neither created nor destroyed. That's the first law of thermodynamics. Around 1850, Rudolf Clausius and William Thomson discovered something that became the basis for the second law. You now know as much about this as I do.

leaders of teams, it is a mandatory one. Consider: If a team leader is not working for the good of the group, he must be working for the good of himself or to whomever he reports. Team members, sensing their leader is not a team player, will one day fly off and leave the team.

If you are a team leader with Teamwork among your signature strengths, you feel a connectedness to the team and a deep engagement with the work of the team. When your team members sense this, they are more willing and eager to be led by you. When you share the responsibility for getting the work done, they feel like you are one of them. Baseball coaches wearing the team uniform look and behave as if they are members of the team. Football coaches often dress like the fans. If someone knows why basketball coaches wear suits and ties, please explain it to me.

Team leaders, use your Teamwork strength to be someone others can depend upon as an active leader of the team. As you do, it will promote respect for your leadership and a willingness to work with you in the future.

LEADING TEAMS WITH YOUR WORK STRENGTHS

Competition®
What do Competition and teams have in common? They both love winning! Competition invigorates teams to do their best, to beat their rivals.

Special purpose teams may be formed to investigate a specific matter, but most teams are formed to do something better than another team elsewhere. This is the nature of competition against others. The members of these teams will use their signature strengths to produce excellence. But the team's success will be measured not by excellence but by how well it performs against an opponent seeking the same result. For such teams, Competition is a great strength to have among the team members and in the leader.

Competition keeps one eye on the prize and the other on the opponent. It measures progress frequently and is quick to respond with a course correction when it will help the team succeed.

When Leading Teams, your Competition provides Stability to the team, one of the four needs of followers. The strong unifying effect that Competition has on team members is a powerful stabilizing force.

Competition is in it to win it. For slackers, a team led by Competition is not a good place to be. For achievers, it is the best place to be. Because winning teams, and winning team members, get prizes. Enough to go around, all thanks to your Leading Teams-Competition competency-strength combo.

Arranger®
Arranger is the strength that discovers the optimal blends of resources and people to achieve a desired result. Arranger looks for, and can see, the effects that different combinations will produce.

The first common goal team members share is to be on a winning team. To mount a sustainable effort, the team embraces diversity to strengthen itself in multiple areas. Who best to match each team member's potential with the position on the team where he or she can make their maximum contribution? Arranger.

Unassigned or, worse, mis-assigned team members can be like loose cannons on the deck of a ship in a storm, casting about and smashing into each other. Thoughtfully assigned team members bring a sense of order to the chaos of life on a high-performing team.

When the game shifts and player changes are called for, Arranger is on it, helping the team rebalance. The Leading Teams-Arranger combo is a handy one to help you keep yor team in balance.

MANAGING CONFLICT

All war is a symptom of man's failure as a thinking animal.
—John Steinbeck

Steinbeck insinuates that the ultimate result of unresolved conflict is war. While we can't eliminate conflict, we can and should move conflict to the background and be mindful it stays there.

Conflict occurs when two or more parties who have different perspectives compete for the same resources. Desired resources may be organic or inorganic, tangible or virtual. Examples include gold, bandwidth, and the hearts and minds of others.

When Leading People, there will always be a certain amount of conflict—conflict between individuals, between teams, between departments. Unresolved conflict dampens productivity and carries with it a heavy load of unnecessary expenses—time lost being unproductive, wasted resources, emotional toil, and the costs of lost opportunities.

Managing Conflict is the process of identifying and reducing disputes. Benefits of Managing Conflict include replacing this impediment to productivity with an understanding of what led to the conflict and better relationships going forward.

Competition can lead to conflict. Thankfully, not all conflicts are symptoms of competition. Therefore, the goal of Managing Conflict is to not produce a "winner," but to find the places where the parties involved can agree on how to work together. When each party has an appreciation for the other's special qualities and challenges, they just might be able to find ways their differences can work for them rather than against them.

When you can manage the amount of conflict in the lives of those you lead, you help people meet their needs for Safety, Trust, Stability, and Hope. People expect a certain amount of conflict when multiple parties are working on the same thing. This is perfectly natural and acceptable *if* you have a way to manage conflicts when they appear. That you are willing and able to Manage Conflict earns you the trust of your followers because they know they can depend upon you to provide a stable environment for them.

THE POTENTIAL FOR CONFLICT

The potential for conflict arises when

- The journey of a person coming from one place and going to another intersects the journey of a person coming from somewhere else and going to a different destination. Fistfight at the oasis!

- Two people are coming from and going to the same place and one person gets in the other's lane. Hey you, outta my way!

- Two people coming from different places do not realize they are trying to get to the same place. This is *my* cab!

A certain amount of tension between different roles is natural. When I was a young VP of marketing for an industrial insurance company, in the office next to me sat the VP of underwriting. I was always having issues with him. He never had issues with me. When I asked the owner of the company about it, he told me "You are *supposed* to have issues. Your jobs are to represent opposing viewpoints." Oh, I get it. Use the accelerator *and* the brakes to get where you want to go. Like I said, I was young.

The primitive choices for ending conflict were fight, flight, fake, or fold.

Fight	Win-lose
Flight	Run away
Fake	Pretend to agree or play dead
Fold	Okay, have it your way

A better option is:

Find	How to use our strengths to manage the conflict

5 STEPS TO MANAGE CONFLICT

Try this straightforward strengths-based approach to improve your Managing Conflict competency:

1   Are both sides willing to end the conflict?

2   Find common ground, a shared goal acceptable to both sides.

3   Name each side's current objectives to achieve the goal. Often, this is where the conflict lives.

4   Name the strengths each uses to achieve their objective.

5   What will it look like when the conflict is resolved?

If I had this conversation with the VP of underwriting, my meeting notes might have looked something like this:

1   This conflict is wasting our time and energy.

2   We are both trying to grow the company.

3   My job is to increase revenue. His job is to increase net income.

4   I use my character strengths Creativity and Zest and my work strengths Strategic and Futuristic to do my job. He uses his character strengths Judgement/ Critical Thinking and his work strengths Analytical and Deliberative to do his.

5   Each of us cannot exist without the other. It is natural that, on occasion, we will disagree.

The loftiest goal of managing conflict: Collaboration.

If you can transform a conflict into an opportunity to work together, you may have found someone to work with in new ways. *If* I had the above conversation with the VP of underwriting, and *if* I had taken advantage of the opportunity to collaborate with my previously imaginary adversary, I would have asked him what classes of business he would like to see *more* of. That would have been powerful information for my marketing messages and sales teams. Alas, I missed the chance.

BE A FACILITATOR

As a leader, people who are unhappy with what others are doing may ask you to choose a side. The role of a judge is to hear both sides and make a decision. Judges don't have to live with the consequences their decisions have on the opposing parties, but leaders do.

A good role for the leader to play in these circumstances is that of facilitator. As a facilitator, your goal is to ensure that the discussions between the parties are as constructive as possible and will enable them to avoid future disputes of a similar nature.

To facilitate conflict resolution, first spend some time with each side. As a guide for your conversation, take each side through the 5 Steps to Manage Conflict. Then bring the parties together and take them through the steps again. It may require several passes but, if you stick with this approach, they will find or create a common ground. They will also come to a greater appreciation of each other's work and the strengths the other person uses to accomplish his goals.

When you sense the onset of resolution, play the devil's advocate—solicit comments on why this will *not* work. At this point, parties who were previously in conflict often use their newfound understanding of the other party and their strengths as a strong case for why it *will* work. When it comes to managing conflict, this is as good as it gets.

When you introduce both sides to the concept of mutual appreciation for each other's strengths, results can include discovery of new ways in which they can work together and a dampening of the potential for future conflicts between them.

* * *

Caveat: Not all conflicts can be resolved.

Some people are just wired in such a way that they annoy you. If your differences are of a superficial or cultural nature, try to overlook them. If your differences stem from opposing values, there may not be much either side can do about it. Just agree to stay out of each other's way when you can.

* * *

Okay, I think you've got this. You now have an uncomplicated 5 Step strengths-based framework to manage conflict and you can put on your Facilitator hat to help others resolve their conflicts. You're not looking for conflict, but when it does come knocking, you'll be ready.

Now let's look at how the character strength Fairness and the work strengths Communication and Individualization could be of assistance to us in Managing Conflict.

MANAGING CONFLICT WITH YOUR CHARACTER STRENGTHS

Fairness®

Those with the strength of Fairness, able to make decisions objectively without preference for their own feelings and opinions, have a talent for managing conflict. As they see the conflict from the outside-in, they exhibit respect for all parties and can promote compromise where it will serve to lessen or resolve the conflict.

Use your Fairness strength to give each party in a conflict, including yourself, the same chance to express his position. When you don't play favorites, others sense that the outcome will be an equitable one.

The value of the strength Fairness lies not in keeping everyone equally happy or unhappy, but in assuring them they will have an honest chance to state their position. When you feel you are doing everything you can to manage a conflict between two people but are getting nowhere, ask one with Fairness how you might change your approach. Sometimes, just being impartial will be enough to encourage others to reduce the differences they perceive between themselves and others.

MANAGING CONFLICT WITH YOUR WORK STRENGTHS

Communication®

Communication, the strength of transmitting messages accurately and convincingly, is a valuable one to have on your side when you are Managing Conflict. Think of Communication as the lubricant that can unstick conflict.

Managing Conflict depends upon Communication to provide a constant and accurate exchange of information between the two parties. There is a name for this: shuttle diplomacy. Shuttle diplomacy, alternating your attention between two disagreeing parties, takes a lot of effort. It is mentally challenging, labor intensive, stressful, and requires deep Communication—the strength *and* the transmission of information. Communicating accurately and often will promote resolution of the conflict and will bring a sense of Trust, one of the needs of people, to the proceedings.

Managing Conflict-Communication, a great competency-strength combo.

Individualization®

Individualization appreciates the unique characteristics of people. Comfortable with the differences between them, Individualization can personalize her relationships with others to bring out the best in them.

Use your Individualization when Managing Conflict to acknowledge the contributions and strengths of both parties—separately at first, then in the presence of each other. When you do so, they will feel acknowledged and their positions better understood. Less defensive, they will begin to understand the contributions and strengths of the other party. When this happens, you will have used your Individualization to bring the conflict to an inflection point—a change in the shape of the trajectory. When the opposing sides begin to feel understood by the neutral party and their opponent, they will begin to relax their positions, often feeling a genuine interest in understanding the other party.

When Individualization helps the door of mutual understanding to open a sliver, you are at the beginning of the end of all the disagreement. Trust will begin to form and a willingness to reach resolution will follow. This little start, and you must be alert to it as it can happen very quickly, is a game changer. Imagine both sides lifting their heads a bit, inhaling, exhaling, then flashing a subtle smile. At this point, you know it can work out.

All this is thanks to Individualization coming to the rescue of Managing Conflicts.

CHAPTER 10

Driving Results

Implementing Your Plans

Some people want it to happen, some wish it would happen,
others make it happen.
—Michael Jordan

THE DRIVING RESULTS COMPETENCIES

TAKING INITIATIVE
EXECUTING EFFICIENTLY

Results are the outcomes brought about by actions.
Driving Results is the category of competencies we employ to implement our plan, guide the process, and produce the outcomes that serve our goals.

Driving Results gives us forward momentum. Without goals and intentional action, nothing will happen in our lives except fortuitous events. Driving Results is what successful people do with their desire to meet the expectations of themselves and others. Doing so, they are the opposite of opportunists, those who only act when they perceive a way to take advantage of a situation.

The competencies of Driving Results are Taking Initiative and Executing Efficiently. Every competency up to this point has prepared us for this moment. Now it's time for us to act with intent and enthusiasm.

Use the Level Up Method to drive your results and close the Gap between your intentions and your impact.

TAKING INITIATIVE

Whatever you can do, or dream you can, begin it.
Boldness has genius, power, and magic in it.
—Goethe[74]

If there is no wind, row.
—Latin proverb

Taking Initiative is beginning a task or a plan of action.

Even when you have a solid strategy and the resources to see it through, starting something can be hard. To take initiative in a new way or on a new thing is not easy. It is especially challenging when, to disrupt the status quo, you have to start from scratch, with no momentum and nothing to build on. It's perfectly natural to feel that your big bang will fizzle. Except that yours won't because you have your Constellation of Competencies, your woven competency-strength combos, to make it happen.

---

74 Johann Wolfgang von Goethe, *Faust.*

A valuable feature of Taking Initiative is that it provides one last chance for reflecting on the competencies and strengths you will consider before acting. A few situations of opportunities for Taking Initiative:

Occurrence	*Your Action*
Something breaks	Find a way to fix it
A new obstacle presents itself	Back the plan up a few steps and revise it
A critical team member is absent	Rearrange the team assignments
A new opportunity presents itself	Focus on your unique ability to seize it

Extra points if you were thinking about which strengths could help you do these things!

Taking Initiative is not a place where we will want to spend a lot of time. It is more of a waypoint than a destination, a place to revisit our plan and gather our focus before we act. Two simple steps will prepare and enable you to take initiative: reconsider your motivation and remove potential barriers to action.

FIRST, RECONSIDER YOUR MOTIVATION...

Like the actor who asks the director, "What's my motivation here?," exploring *why* you are doing something before you act will inform you how to play your role. Understanding what you want to achieve and why you want to achieve it will help you choose which strengths to call upon to produce the desired effect. Periodically reminding yourself of what first motivated you will help you act in the ways most beneficial to achieving your goal.

Reflect a bit on the source of your motivation. Is it intrinsic or extrinsic?

Intrinsic motivation arises from within and produces a desire to do something that will be personally fulfilling. Those who are intrinsically motivated often cite their pursuit of excellence. The things you do just because you want to are those you are motivated intrinsically to do. You willingly, often eagerly, prepare yourself—studying and practicing—to engage in these activities. The result may be personal growth, a sense of accomplishment, or simply enjoyment. What does Taking Initiative look like when it is the response to intrinsic motivation? As an example, let's say you want to write a short story for your own amusement. You may:

1   ponder a few subjects and pick one
2   consider from what point of view you will write
3   check out how-to websites and books, and examples of this kind of writing
4   join a writers' group for support
5   pick the personal resources you will use to write the story
6   sit down to a blank screen or a sheet of paper
7   begin writing

Look at all the steps you took on the way to starting your story. Q: Where could you say you were Taking Initiative? A: At every step until the final one. At that point, when you put pen to paper or tapped the first keystroke, you were Executing. Efficiently, we assume. Because you planned well and took initiative, you were *prepared* to act.

Extrinsic motivation comes from outside us. Among extrinsic motivators are the consequences that we produce. Potential for reward or punishment are common extrinsic motivators. So much of life is extrinsically motivated. Children attend school because their parents expect them to, adults work to provide food and shelter, and some people do things just to test themselves against others.

The children in class, the runner in the race, the worker on the assembly line, and the chess player in the tournament—all are measured against their peers, all are extrinsically motivated.

On the path to your vision, you will encounter both intrinsic and extrinsic motivators. Q: Which type is preferable? A: Whichever kind gives you the best opportunity to use and enjoy your signature strengths as you make progress. Intellectuals tend to be intrinsically motivated. Professional athletes deeply understand extrinsic motivation. The rest of us are somewhere in between, depending on the opportunities available and how we define success.

...THEN, REMOVE BARRIERS TO ACTION

You've considered, studied, reviewed, and pondered the big issues. You've developed a plan and gained support for it from the major stakeholders. Yet something is keeping you from moving to GO. You are still "fixin' to get ready." It's time to address and clean up those lingering barriers to Taking Initiative.

Common barriers include:

- Conflicting priorities: Resolve them now. Quickly. They had their chance.

- Too many choices: Narrow them down to three, then one. The time for thinking was the past. Now is the time for doing. Too many choices and self-doubt are the two most oft-cited reasons for inaction.

- Distractions: Put them on hold. If they hang up, you can call them back. Or not.

- Fear of Failure: With your strengths and competencies, not even possible!

When you've reconsidered your motivation and removed barriers to action, you're ready to take initiative. Here's a little encouragement from someone who is comfortable with literally starting with a blank page:[75]

> *You can, you should, and*
> *if you're brave enough to start, you will.*
> —Stephen King

Now let's consider how the character strengths Hope and Leadership and two very different work strengths, Activator and

---

75 No planning, story arcs, and plot development for Stephen King. He just starts writing. Really.

Restorative, could be beneficial to us when Taking Initiative.

TAKING INITIATIVE WITH YOUR CHARACTER STRENGTHS

Hope®

In my seventh-grade catechism class, I was assigned this motto:

Faith is the assurance of things hoped for, the conviction of things not seen.
—Hebrews 11:1

I had no idea what it meant. Maybe that's why it was given to me, or maybe because my birthday was 11/1? Today, I know exactly what it means. Hope and faith are inextricably linked. And I am a very hopeful person. (Hope is my #4 character strength.)

Hope, the strength that gives us positive expectations for what may come, encourages us to take those first steps toward the future.

Use your strength of Hope to take your first steps and take initiative. Engaging your Hope will promote optimism in yourself and those around you. When you and others feel optimistic, you will believe that what you do will help things to turn out well.

Paralysis by analysis, mentioned earlier, is a common barrier for those who are finding it difficult to take initiative. If you are one of them, engage someone who has Hope among his signature strengths to help you think things through. As he does so, you may begin to see "how things will work out for the good despite obstacles along the way."[76]

---

76 Ryan M. Niemiec and Robert E. McGrath, *The Power of Character Strengths* (Cincinnati, OH: Via Institute on Character, 2019), 243.

Leadership®

The first thing great leaders do is not mobilize others and induce them to act. The first thing great leaders do is create a vision and organize others in a way that will best support them working with one another to achieve the goals. In doing so, they use their strength of Leadership to take the initiative now that will drive results later.

You can use your Leadership strength to help you take initiative as you address these five steps.

1. First, consider the places you could go with what you have or could acquire. Pick the best one. That's your vision.

2. Next, examine all the combinations of your resources that could take you toward your vision. Pick the best one. That's your organization.

3. Now, think of ways your organization could move toward your vision. Pick the best ones. These are your goals.

4. Next, contemplate how groups of people could best accomplish the goals. Those are your teams.

5. Finally, identify the best people for each team and gain their membership and support.

If, before you read this, you thought taking initiative would be far easier than executing, welcome to the club. The activities that comprise taking initiative present great opportunities to use our Leadership strength.

If you are perfectly positioned for takeoff at the upwind end of a runway in your life but don't feel ready to throttle up, ask someone with Leadership to go through your checklist with you. He can help you confirm that you are going where you want to go, you have the navigational aids and aircraft to do so, the tanks are topped off, and the crew is trained and motivated to do their part on the flight. Then you can radio the cabin, "Prepare for takeoff!"

TAKING INITIATIVE WITH YOUR WORK STRENGTHS

Activator®

Activator, the strength that makes things happen, is a powerful initiator. Activator is always on the lookout for opportunities to act.

Activator lives in that small space between thinking and acting. What else lives in the small space between thinking and acting? Yes, Taking Initiative! Use Activator when Taking Initiative to shorten the time between your thinking and your acting. When you are truly ready, Activator will be the first strength to know it.

When you or your team wishes to begin a journey, enlist an Activator to get started. Activator will quickly help you move the conversation from where do we start? to when can we start?

Restorative®

Things will break. It happens. When they do, you can spend a lot of time investigating the cause and evaluating the options. Even after doing so, it can be difficult to choose the best way to begin the repairs. This is what Restorative does. Restorative loves finding ways to fix things that are broken. Restorative can identify what caused the breakdown and initiate a plan to fix it. Restorative knows that broken is a temporary state. Restorative, moving calmly and methodically, can be a fine strength to help you get things back into working order and moving again.

A bit of a stealth strength, Restorative waits calmly for something to break so he can repair it. When we desperately need something to be fixed, Restorative is the one that can assess what must be done and begin the process to set things right again. Opportunities for Restorative to take initiative include determining the cause of a production line disruption, assisting a team member with his productivity after a long leave of absence, and helping the organization regain its place in the market after a PR setback. One example we can all relate to: the customer service rep who has a genuine interest in getting our issue resolved and their service to us restored. When our credit card is denied, our computer crashes, or our car grinds to a halt on the highway, it's panic time. How thankful are we when the person on the other end of the line gives us assurance that he will resolve our issue? Thank you, Restorative, for Taking Initiative!

When your things break, engage your Restorative or find a Restorative to collaborate with.

Restorative, initiating a plan to fix things, will provide a sense of regained forward motion.

EXECUTING EFFICIENTLY

Vision without execution is hallucination.
—Thomas A. Edison

Executing Efficiently is putting your plans into effect.

You've prepared yourself to execute efficiently—to use everything you've got to get something done in a competent manner. Thinking Strategically, you created the vision, set the goals, and developed the plan to achieve them. Navigating Change, you calculated the risks and anticipated the need to communicate frequently throughout the process. Leading People, you built quality relationships with the individuals and the teams you will work with to achieve the objectives. You're prepared for the likely eventualities. When life happens, you will be able to identify the competencies best suited to address a problem, apply your signature strengths to the competencies, and resolve the issue. You have taken the first step to initiate action and are now ready to Execute Efficiently, to advance from your goals to your achievements.

Taking responsibility to achieve something adds meaning to our lives and gives us a sense of purpose.

Executing Efficiently is where you get to merge and activate the three components of any successful venture: your strategy, the people, and the process.

Executing is *action*—the night of the annual gala for the museum after a year of planning, the day of competition for the athlete, the performance for the musician, the trial for the lawyer, the IPO for the entrepreneur, and the launch day of any meaningful project in your life.

You are now well prepared to act on your plans in your way. Here are a few tips to take with you and ways to use your competency-strength combos to keep you going:

THE 5 KEY ELEMENTS OF EXECUTING EFFICIENTLY

1 Vision First

Work only on goals that will engage your signature strengths to form the competency-strength combos that will take you closer to realizing your vision. Encourage others to do the same. Be mindful that everything else is a pleasant diversion, a distraction, or a hobby. Your competency-strength combos are the fuel in your tank. They will take you the distance, to your vision.

2 Timing is Everything

Set your priorities and use your competency-strength combos to work on the right projects at the right time. To keep your focus tight, work on no more than three significant priorities at a time. Schedule out the lesser ones and those that can wait. Out-of-sequence work, no matter how successful, makes a weaker contribution to reaching a goal than doing the right thing at the right time.

3 Use Your Relationships

You built your collaborative relationships for a reason. Now is when you make productive use of them. Collaborating with others who have different strengths and competencies will amplify your abilities. When you do so, you provide opportunities for their personal development and strengthen your relationships with them.

4 Stay Results-oriented
Organize and work on every project in a way that harnesses your competency-strength combos to achieve the objectives. When you drift off course, or a new goal will better serve the vision than the current goal, correct your course. Planning intermediate wins and celebrating them will sustain your momentum.

5 Show Up and Do the Work
Have you seen the Immaculate Heart College Art Department rules?[77]

They are wonderful!

The first time through, read them just as they appear on the page.

Here they are:

---

77 Sister Corita Kent, with collaboration from composer John Cage, for a class she taught 1967–68 at Immaculate Heart Convent, Los Angeles.

IMMACULATE HEART COLLEGE ART DEPARTMENT RULES

Rule 1 FIND A PLACE YOU TRUST AND THEN
TRY TRUSTING IT FOR A WHILE

Rule 2 GENERAL DUTIES OF A STUDENT
PULL EVERYTHING OUT OF YOUR TEACHER
PULL EVERYTHING OUT OF YOUR FELLOW STUDENTS

Rule 3 GENERAL DUTIES OF A TEACHER
PULL EVERYTHING OUT OF YOUR STUDENTS

Rule 4 CONSIDER EVERYTHING AN EXPERIMENT

Rule 5 BE SELF DISCIPLINED. THIS MEANS
FINDING SOMEONE WISE OR SMART AND
CHOOSING TO FOLLOW THEM.
TO BE DISCIPLINED IS TO FOLLOW IN A GOOD WAY
TO BE SELF DISCIPLINED IS TO FOLLOW IN A BETTER WAY

Rule 6 NOTHING IS A MISTAKE. THERE'S NO WIN AND
NO FAIL THERE'S ONLY MAKE

Rule 7 The only rule is work.
IF YOU WORK IT WILL LEAD TO SOMETHING
IT'S THE PEOPLE WHO DO ALL OF THE WORK ALL THE TIME
WHO EVENTUALLY CATCH ON TO THINGS

Rule 8 DON'T TRY TO CREATE AND ANALYSE AT THE
SAME TIME. THEY'RE DIFFERENT PROCESSES

Rule 9 BE HAPPY WHENEVER YOU CAN MANAGE IT
ENJOY YOURSELF IT'S LIGHTER THAN YOU
THINK

Rule 10 "WE'RE BREAKING ALL OF THE RULES. EVEN
OUR OWN RULES. AND HOW DO WE DO THAT?
BY LEAVING PLENTY OF ROOM FOR X QUANTITIES." JOHN CAGE

HELPFUL HINTS: ALWAYS BE AROUND. COME OR GO TO EVERY-
THING ALWAYS GO TO CLASSES. READ ANYTHING YOU CAN GET
YOUR HANDS ON. LOOK AT MOVIES CAREFULLY, OFTEN
SAVE EVERYTHING-IT MIGHT COME IN HANDY LATER
THERE SHOULD BE NEW RULES NEXT WEEK

On a second reading, substitute *follower* for *student*, *leader* for *teacher*, and *continue to learn* for *go to classes*. Even better!

Take some time with these. They are all good. Each one is encouraging, reaffirming, and challenging at once. My favorites are:

Rule #7   The only rule is work. If you work, it will lead to something.

Helpful Hints   Always be around. Come or go to everything.

There it is—show up…and do the work.

Another gem from Thomas Edison:

Opportunity is missed by most people because it is dressed in overalls and looks like work.

Success isn't the goal, doing the work is the goal.
Success is *the result* of doing the work.

As Maya Angelou said, "Nothing will work unless you do."

So, after all your preparations, how to execute is quite straightforward—work. Can you do the work? You can. That's what your strengths and competencies are for—to help you do the work that will lead to your success. Soon it will be you saying, *The harder I work, the luckier I get.*

Like the volume knob on amplifiers, lists of rules usually stop at 10. But if this list had one more, it might be:

Rule #11: Use your Strengths and Competencies. They were for work made.

Now let's see how the character strength Zest and four work strengths—Achiever, Deliberative, Focus, and Responsibility—might be used to help us Execute Efficiently.

EXECUTING EFFICIENTLY WITH YOUR CHARACTER STRENGTHS

Zest®

Those with the strength of Zest go about getting stuff done with energy and enthusiasm. They do things wholeheartedly and feel alive and excited by what they can achieve.

When you use your strength of Zest, you can more fully engage yourself in your endeavors. As you do so, you will sense that your life is more fulfilling, meaningful, and purposeful.

If you are considering how to add some new concepts to your life or how to offer them to others with whom you accomplish things, ask someone with Zest for his perspective on how to do so. His enthusiasm to explore and embrace new concepts may energize you to bring some excitement to how you and others can use your new ideas.

EXECUTING EFFICIENTLY WITH YOUR WORK STRENGTHS

Achiever®

Achiever executes. That's what he does. Not one to rest on his laurels, Achiever starts every day at zero and measures his progress at the end of every day.

The one who is already *doing* when the rest of us are just *arriving*? Achiever. And he's happy about it. Even on Monday. The one who comes to meetings eager to accomplish something? Again, Achiever.

When your or your team's project begins to lose speed, enlist an Achiever to work alongside you. He will find things that can be done in the direction of the goals, and he will begin to do them. This will re-energize you and the team and, before you know it, you will again be underway, Executing Efficiently.

Deliberative®

Unsure of the best path to reach your goal? Engage Deliberative to assist with a careful evaluation of your options. The result will be executing with the certainty that comes from thorough consideration. Contrast Deliberative with Activator:

Activator	Ready-Fire-Aim
Deliberative	Ready-Aim, Aim, Aim-Fire

When you gotta move *now*, Activator is the way to go.

When the sequence of your actions will benefit from assessing the options, Deliberative can do.

Imagine you are on a project with a tight deadline. The usual reaction is, we have to hurry up, right? Yes, but consider the counterintuitive approach Deliberative can bring: "If we're behind schedule, we better get this right the first time, as there will be no time to come back and fix it if we get it wrong." Oh, we hadn't thought of that. Thank you, Deliberative.

If your project has many variables, Deliberative can thoughtfully examine each and help you execute in the most efficient way.

Focus®

Focus, with his long attention span, can help you maintain your concentration on the things that will most help you execute efficiently as you work on your goal.

We've all witnessed and admired people who do their thing with no wasted motion. The "in the zone" NFL quarterback, the professional pool player, and the tai chi class on the lawn beneath your hotel room window. They are…focused.

When you need to confine your actions to the ones that will help you achieve your desired goals, engage your Focus or partner with someone who has Focus among his signature strengths.

Responsibility®

Executing Efficiently, like all activities, is divided into three stages: starting, doing, and finishing. Responsibility, the strength of dependability, comes in during the doing, sees it through to finishing, and turns the lights off after everyone else has gone home. Responsibility has a deep sense of loyalty to the obligations he assumes. When finishing strong is of utmost importance, engage Responsibility to add a level of commitment to achieving the best possible result.

Say the business you are in is a fast-paced, competitive one. (What business isn't!) You like the focus required by a marketplace in constant motion. The never-ending chain of urgent deadlines, not so much. But here you are again, at the end of another product development cycle, with marketing and the front office at your door asking for your work. They advise you, "Don't let great be the enemy of good." Yes, but if you release this piece of you-know-what to the marketplace, you know there will be consequences. Enter Responsibility. He calmly points out that the product in its current state of development does not match what was promised. If we can't keep our promises, who will we be? A rhetorical question and a wake-up call all in one. Responsibility reminds us that *we* are not at the third stage, finishing, until the *product* is there. Until such time as it is, we are going to keep working to deliver what was promised. Responsibility's inner dependability just added an external feature to you and your project—trustworthiness.

Use Responsibility to take ownership of your results. As you do so, you will be executing more efficiently and delivering the results you promised yourself, your team, and your customers. And others will be inspired to do the same.

CHAPTER 11

Developing Self

Bettering Yourself

Make the most of yourself, for that is all there is of you.
—Ralph Waldo Emerson

THE DEVELOPING SELF COMPETENCIES

CONTINUALLY LEARNING
ACTING PROFESSIONALLY
CONTINOUSLY IMPROVING

Developing Self is consciously taking steps to better oneself. In the preceding chapters we looked *outward,* forming and improving the competencies to help us productively think and do. We now look *inward,* to three competencies that will aid the ongoing expansion of our abilities to tackle the topics of interest in our lives. These competencies are just for you.

Successful people toggle between developing themselves and action, using their increased capacity to address the issues that matter.

If you are a high achiever, self-development is crucial to maintaining your edge to capably address what the future will bring. If you are not yet a high achiever, with self-development you can create the tools and proficiently use them to become one. Each of our categories of competencies provides unique benefits.

Developing Self

- Gives you new resources to improve your other competencies.

- Prepares you to create new competency-strength combinations.

- Encourages you to map your progress.

- Boosts your self-awareness and confidence.

- Increases your capacity to Level Up.

Think of Developing Self as your voluntary and ongoing intervention. To make way for your new ways of thinking and acting, you will be discarding some of the old ones. Another benefit of Developing Self: For some reason, throwing out old stuff just *feels* good.

Developing Self: Do it for yourself and do it for your competencies.

Why do some mid-career professionals take time and effort to seek advanced degrees? Is it for the knowledge? Sometimes. Is it to increase their confidence and sense of self-worth? Always. When those you know are working to better themselves, congratulate them on the taking the initiative and making the effort to improve. If they are on your side in the game, you can also thank them for doing so.

One final benefit of Developing Self: *It inspires others to develop themselves.*

A world in which we are all trying to be better versions of ourselves is a good one.

Think of a time when you used some new knowledge or skill to do something better than before. It felt good, right? If we want more of the little pick-me-ups we get from bringing the new into our lives, all we need to do is continue developing ourselves.

As we improve, we experience increased confidence, a more meaningful life, and greater success. In addition to these benefits, improving also decreases possibilities on the downside. Creating and maintaining momentum in our lives tamps down the potential for stalls and derailments—the two leading causes of career malaise and feeling less vital. Using your competency-strength combos will contribute to you feeling very vital!

Success is often measured by how one meets one's real or imagined needs or how one compares oneself to others. Among those who are extrinsically motivated, success might be a $25 million beachfront cottage in the Hamptons *and* a jet. Wow is right. Success can also be measured by the level of excellence one achieves. To one who is intrinsically motivated, success might be getting a PhD in a field other than her occupation. Wow again. Now that we have covered the outliers, we can focus on how we define success for ourselves.

Take a moment to consider what will give you a sense of living a more meaningful, more successful life. Don't be too hard on yourself; you can always move the bar up later. Moving the bar down is no fun.

That bar way up there? That's your vision. Your goals are much closer to the ground. They can be reached by using your unique strengths and your competencies. Accomplishing your goals will take you in the direction of your vision.

Define your own success in a way that is both achievable and upgradable. Maybe start with this:

A successful person is one who uses his strengths to accomplish goals and intentionally improves himself in a way that creates meaning in his life.

Deceptive, this little definition. It sounds straightforward, but how many people actually do it?

You do. You already know how to use your strengths in ways that will improve your outward-facing competencies. As you do so, you become more capable and confident in your thoughts and actions. Adding the inward-facing competencies of Developing Self will help you create additional capacity and boost your self-confidence.

Confidence, the belief in one's own abilities, is a key ingredient of success. For leaders to be effective, confidence is essential.

Can you be successful if you are not confident? Yes, but if you intentionally use your strengths to improve your outward-

and inward-facing competencies, you *will* be confident. And successful. These four are inextricably linked:

STRENGTHS →
    COMPETENCIES →
        CONFIDENCE→
            SUCCESS

Take away one, and the others will fade. A little or a lot.

Confidence is one of the cornerstones of success at all levels. With confidence, you can:

- Effectively and enthusiastically communicate your vision.

- Present yourself as self-assured.

- Make better decisions and act with the information you have.

- Maintain your sense of humor.

A confident leader, with his sense of calm and the ability to make quality decisions, has the effect of making other people feel more sure of themselves. His ongoing self-development prepares him to continue doing so in the future, when the challenges will certainly be different than those of today.

This reserve of confidence does not come to a leader by accident or by birth. High achievers develop the competencies of Continually Learning, Acting Professionally, and Continuously Improving one day at a time.

CONTINUALLY LEARNING

Chance favors a prepared mind.
—Louis Pasteur

Continually Learning involves periodically and frequently acquiring new skills and knowledge to respond more effectively to challenges and opportunities.

When we learn, we grow. Continually Learning prepares us to successfully adapt to the changing demands in our lives.

Unattributable but great aphorisms on learning include: "The more you know the more you grow" and, even better, "The more you know, the more you know you don't know." Not really from Aristotle, no matter what the poster says.

Learning is like going to school, right? Not really. Check out these fine observations by George Couros, a wizard on the subject of learning:[78]

- School promotes starting by looking for answers.
  Learning promotes starting with questions.

- School is about finding information on something prescribed to you.
  Learning is about exploring your passions and interests.

---

78 George Couros, "School vs. Learning," The Principle of Change blog, December 27, 2014, https://georgecouros.ca/blog/archives/4974.

- Schools teach compliance.
  Learning is about challenging perceived norms.
  School is standardized.
  Learning is personal.

- School teaches us to obtain information from certain people.
  Learning promotes that everyone is a teacher, and everyone is a learner.

- School promotes surface-level thinking.
  Learning is about deep exploration.

Once we've graduated from credentialed channels of learning, we determine what we'll learn, how we'll learn it, and at what pace. The key to continually learning is to make it a habit. ABL: Always Be Learning. If you do so, you will not only improve your perspectives, you will also discover new occasions to use your strengths and competencies. That right there is the case for Continually Learning.

7+ BENEFITS OF CONTINUALLY LEARNING

Continually Learning means making outlays to secure a larger stake in a blue-chip investment: our future selves. In return for the contributions of our time, effort, and inquisitiveness, we receive some nice dividends:

1 New insights and broader perspectives
2 Ability to think more comprehensively
3 Current knowledge on trends that may affect us
4 Better preparation for new challenges
5 Learning new concepts promotes the creation of new ideas

6　Rise in our value, to ourselves and others

And, saving the best for last,

7　Increased self-confidence

Another great benefit of Continually Learning is how much stronger it makes our signature strengths. For example, let's see how learning might amplify the character strengths Honesty and Spiritualty and two very different work strengths, Analytical and Empathetic.

Because adults learn when and what they want to learn, and because using our strengths is pleasing, we tend to voluntarily learn things that will be in keeping with how we naturally think, feel, and act.

- One with the character strength Honesty will pursue learning that helps him be more authentic.

- And one with the character strength Spirituality will seek to learn more about how he can connect with his higher purpose.

- One with work strength Analytical will gravitate to learning that helps him perform better assessments.

- And one with the work strength Empathy will happily immerse herself in new information that informs her ability to better understand others.

Continually Learning—a natural strengths booster.

A casual style of occasional learning, where you pick up pieces of this and that, is okay. But *directional* learning is more likely to achieve the leveling-up that you want in your life. The question is often, "How do I determine the curriculum for my life to get me where I want to go?" Try this exercise to reveal topics worthy of your further exploration:

Look–	*to learn something that will help you–*
Inward	Be a better person in some way
Outward	Be of greater value to others
Backward	Remedy a suboptimal capability
Forward	Prepare for the future

There is no right way to learn. Investigate any topic between you and your vision of yourself and the inevitable result will be some self-development. The only must-do is ABL...always be learning!

Let's see how the character strengths Curiosity and Love of Learning and the work strengths Learner and Context can help us to be Continually Learning.

CONTINUALLY LEARNING WITH YOUR CHARACTER STRENGTHS

Curiosity®

Those with the strength of Curiosity love to acquire new information, new experiences, and new friends. They are open to concepts, activities, and people that offer them opportunities for investigation and inspiration.

Use your strength of Curiosity to support your quest to be continually learning. One way Curiosity can help us learn more about anything or anyone is by starting with "why?"[79]

A great reason to use your Curiosity in this way lies in the name of the site Curiosity Makes You Smarter.[80] Their many articles and podcasts have titles like "Sleep vs. Exercise: Which is More Important?" that will pique almost anyone's interest. One thing is for sure, the people at Curiosity and everyone who benefits from their observations are continually learning.

When you find you are losing interest in something you are working on, ask someone with Curiosity among his signature strengths to help you discover why. As you begin to take apart what is behind your sense of disconnection, you may discover new reasons and new ways to reaffirm your commitment to your project. Or you may find that you are drifting away from it for good reason. Either way, Curiosity can get you on the path to discovering the answer.

Love of Learning®
We instinctively know that the strength Love of Learning improves our competency to be Continually Learning. Let's see if we can discover something new here.

---

79 If "starting with why" sounds familiar, it may be because you have seen the terrific Simon Sinek TED talk "Start with Why" from 2009. Viewed by 30 million people, it is subtitled in 43 languages and is the third-most watched talk of all time
80 Curiosity is an online education website that was spun off from the Discovery Channel. You can find it by going to www.curiosity.com

Continually learning may be motivated by an external force. In the US, our K-12 education system is funded by state and local governments at the level of $1.2 trillion per year. Compulsory school attendance varies by state. It starts between ages 5 and 7 and continues until ages 16 to 19. After high school, our employers may require us to take their mandatory training sessions.

More often, continually learning is motivated by internal forces. People of every age have hobbies and acquire skills to think in ways they find interesting and do things in which they have an interest. Those with the strength Love of Learning may learn just for the mental stimulation and pleasure that learning new things brings them. Or they may find joy in acquiring new and deeper understandings of things they can use in their everyday lives.

If you are feeling as if you don't have the answers to solve a problem you have, ask one with Love of Learning among her signature strengths to join your investigation. She may help you see that not knowing the answers to things is a perfectly acceptable situation, one that is easily remedied by...learning!

CONTINUALLY LEARNING WITH YOUR WORK STRENGTHS

Learner®

Learner is the strength of inquisitiveness. We can all learn. Learner loves the *process* of acquiring new information. If you have Learner among your signature strengths, you naturally seek out opportunities to discover new things. The one with the stack of unread nonfiction books on his bedside table, scores of links to favorite TED Talks and Kahn Academy classes, and a calendar full of webinars? Typical Learner!

For Learner, Continually Learning is automatic. For the rest of us, we can take inspiration from the zeal with which a Learner dives into the exploration of the new. Mirroring the behavior of others can be one of the best shortcuts to self-improvement. Think about how you first learned to throw a ball. Did you read the instructions before you attempted it? Unlikely. You probably watched a kid who knew what he was doing, and then you tried to do it like he did. Eventually, it worked. Same here. With a Learner nearby, we can witness and appreciate the joy he takes in expanding his knowledge base and let some of his enthusiasm rub off on us. Then we will be the ones Continually Learning as we eagerly look for information on ways we can better think and act.

Context®

Context, drawing lessons from the past, can increase the effectiveness of Continually Learning. Think of Context and Futuristic as bringing different time dimensions to the present. As Futuristic brings the vision of the future to the present, Context brings the lessons from the past to the present:

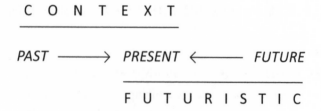

You've probably heard Winston Churchill's "Those who fail to learn from history are condemned to repeat it." Context is what Churchill was referring to. By bringing to the present what we have learned from the past, Context adds an element of efficiency to our learning. Context allows us to *start* with that which is known, saving us the expenses associated with relearning it. With Context in the room, we can apply ourselves to learning *new* things. When we don't have to interrupt our learning with detours to research the past for answers, we improve our ability to be *Continually* Learning.

ACTING PROFESSIONALLY

A professional is someone who can do his best work when he doesn't feel like it.
—Alistair Cooke

Acting Professionally means being approachable, resourceful, dependable, and good at what you do. Acting Professionally will help any high achiever Level Up faster. When you act more professionally, you become the go-to person, the one everyone trusts—not only to get the job done, but to admirably represent your team and the organization.

7 BENEFITS OF ACTING PROFESSIONALLY

Acting Professionally is another of our free-range competencies. It has a nice multiplier effect on the impact of everything we do. Acting Professionally, we gain:

1 Better relationships with our coworkers, our superiors, and our customers
2 Ability to more effectively demonstrate our other competencies, especially Inspiring Others and Influencing Others
3 Increased self-confidence

4   Greater credibility
5   More respect and an increase in our perceived value
6   Added luster to our achievements
7   Forgiveness of small missteps

Imagine you will hire one of two candidates. Both are high achievers. They are different people but score identical in terms of their qualifications for the position. The difference is that one acts more professionally than the other. You know where this is going. The rest of this little scenario writes itself. If we had to reduce our case for Acting Professionally down to one compelling motive, it would be simply to see and seize more opportunities.

THE 7 INGREDIENTS OF ACTING PROFESSIONALLY

There is a lot of talk in the professional development world about personal brand, executive presence, and being authentic. Each of them exhibits a subset of the characteristics of Acting Professionally. Why not go for *all* the ingredients of Acting Professionally and get every one of these descriptors as collateral benefits?

Here they are, seven simple ways you can be perceived as Acting Professionally:

1   Be positive
2   Be friendly
3   Be self-aware
4   Live your values
5   Put your strengths and competencies to productive use

6   Do the work
7   Remain resilient

To incrementally improve your professionalism, work on improving these one at a time. To act thoroughly professionally, display all seven. Do so and you will be perceived as open, honest, and effective.

John Baldoni powerfully sets out the two best suggestions to help us achieve all seven:[81]

> Watch what you say. Words do matter.
> Watch what you do. Actions speak louder than words.

A few thoughts on our final ingredient of Acting Professionally:

REMAIN RESILIENT...

Being resilient means possessing the ability to withstand or recover quickly from difficult situations. When a challenge comes along, the fresher you are, the better able you are to deal with it, right? We use our competency-strength combos to get things done and put them to bed so they don't clutter our lives. But life is a complex affair. Do you ever get the feeling that your life is in charge of you? The more successful we become, the more lingering issues we carry into the next day. No matter what we do, we will never be able to control everything. If we could, uncertainty wouldn't be the prominent fixture that makes our lives so interesting. When you use the Level Up Method to take charge of your life, you will reduce a significant contributor to stress: doubt that you will be able to perform in an effective way.

---

81 John Baldoni, *Lead with Purpose* (New York: AMACOM, 2012).

...AVOID BROWNOUT

We know that extended overwhelm can lead to burnout. When our friends, family, bosses, or coworkers—anyone who is concerned for our well-being—urge us to take it easy, we should listen to what they're trying to tell us. True burnout, a total shutdown resulting from prolonged and unattended overextension, is the extreme case. The warning signs are rolling blackouts, loss of effectiveness in one or more parts of our lives, or, more frequently, brownouts. When we suffer a brownout, everything gets darker and our lives dim from the mental, emotional, or physical overload.

During a brownout, our productivity and quality of life plummet, but we keep shuffling about like zombies. Tip:

Almost everything will work again if you unplug it for a few minutes...including you.
—Anne Lamott

When you feel the onset of a brownout in your life, take a step back. Think about one and only one productive, rewarding, and easily achievable thing you can do with just one pretested competency-strength combo. Push everything else from your focus for the next hour or two. What is smaller than a small win? A micro win. That is what you are going for. When you get your micro win, do a little something for yourself. Immediately. Uber to the park and sit on a bench, buy a magazine on a topic of interest and duck into a café. Give yourself a little boost, like the one your phone receives when you give it a quick recharge at the airport between your flights.

There, you just learned a new application of your competency-strength combos: Not only can they be used to facilitate things you want to happen, they can also be used to diminish the impact of things you *don't* want to occur, like a weakening of your resiliency that could affect your ability to act professionally.

We now explore how the character strength Self-Regulation and two work strengths Belief and Woo can support our Acting Professionally.

ACTING PROFESSIONALLY WITH YOUR CHARACTER STRENGTHS

Self-Regulation®

A big part of acting professionally is behaving in a controlled and stable manner. Those with the strength of Self-Regulation can think and perform in the measured ways we associate with acting professionally.

Use your strength of Self-Regulation to improve your study habits when you wish to learn new things, your behavior when you wish to convey to others that you are dependable, and your appetite to gain a sense of self-control.

The strength Self-Regulation is deep and wide, one which cannot be done justice in so small a space as this. An overly general and overly brief summary might be that with some discipline, each of us should be able to practice some self-restraint.

If you are preparing for a presentation, anything from a toast to the newlyweds to presenting a scientific paper, ask one with Self-Regulation for his opinion. He may help you see that enthusiasm is a great thing, but that it can be more effective when communicated with a bit of subtlety. There, with one swipe, you just added some professionalism to your presentation.

ACTING PROFESSIONALLY WITH YOUR WORK STRENGTHS

Belief®

Belief, with its keen sense of what is right, is a strength naturally aligned with Acting Professionally. Belief not only knows right from wrong; she also draws upon her values to nourish her as she lives her life with purpose. When she does so, she displays a truly genuine way of Acting Professionally.

Those with Belief live the core values that give their lives meaning. They honor them and naturally align their actions with them. When they do so, they exhibit both a sense of commitment to their deeply held principles and the durability to remain true to them.

When you wish to improve your professionalism but need some internal motivation to do so, talk with someone you admire who has Belief among her signature strengths. She will help you see the unseen and revitalize your commitment to your values. As you find ways to express your commitments to your principles, you will be perceived as Acting more Professionally.

Woo®

Woo, Winning Others Over, launches the Acting Professionally process fast. Woo, always self-aware, leads with positivity and is sincerely friendly. Woo exudes warmth and professionalism by connecting and showing a genuine interest in others. On a team, the work of Woo is not to shoulder the entire Acting Professionally burden alone. Rather, Woo's contribution comes early, making strong positive first impressions that help set the stage for what is to come.

Imagine you are hosting a two-day off-site retreat for the executives of a large client. Significant others are invited, and you have planned activities for them while your meetings are in session. Considerable planning and expense have gone into making the arrangements for this event, and you are gratified the clients have allocated their precious time to attend. This is a big opportunity for you, your team, and your organization. The cocktail reception the night before the event is your chance to get off on the right foot, to set the tone for the next two days. How to do so, to demonstrate just the right combination of cordiality and professionalism? Easy. Identify a he and a she Woo from your team and give them free rein as your greeters. Those with Woo live for opportunities like this. They will effortlessly and graciously welcome the guests, introduce them to one another, set a positive mood, and keep the conversations going during the reception. With Woo on the job, relationships between those who are new to one another will be off to a good start. And the evening will pave the way for a positive response to your presentations during the retreat.

When you wish to make a convivial and professional first impression, engage your Woo or enlist one with Woo to help you do so.

CONTINOUSLY IMPROVING

I must be willing to give up what I am
in order to become what I will be.
—Albert Einstein

Continuously Improving is voluntarily making steady and incremental progress, not only in gaining new knowledge, as we do when we are Continually Learning, but also in improving ourselves. Fortunately, the bedrock assumption of Continuously Improving is that the gains will be incremental. Radical innovation requires significant investment, carries a high degree of risk, and seeks to completely replace the existing. Most of us really don't want to replace ourselves. Instead, and this is the book in a nutshell:

Seek to make small but intentional improvements in the direction
of your vision and goals and you will Level Up to close the Gap.

When organizations refer to Continuous Improvement (CI), they are referencing their ongoing efforts to reduce internal waste and improve the quality of their processes, products, or services. For some reason, the approaches they take to achieve this often have daunting names, like Kaizen, Lean, Agile, and Six Sigma.

Don't worry, nowhere here will we ask *you* to be "lean." Quite the opposite. Level Up is all about using your strengths to improve your competencies and become *abundant*. You will have *more* of what you need to take you where you want to go.

What we will ask you to do is to take yourself out of your comfort zone when it will help you improve your performance.

Here is a simple, straightforward approach to initiate the continuous improvement in your life:

Pick a subject of interest or importance on any topic and ask yourself, "How could I make this better in some small way?" If nothing immediately comes to mind, grab our list of competencies, pick one, and be ready for the flood of ideas you will generate on things you could improve.

Toward the end of this chapter, we'll provide a guide for you to do this exercise. But for now, just imagine taking a few minutes every week to identify some minor but meaningful thing to improve.

In time, you will have a collection of small things that are now better. What do we do with collections of similar ingredients? We combine them! Think of a delicious meal, an exhibition in an art museum, a symphony orchestra, or a new car rolling off the assembly line. Each of them came into being one small thing at a time.

This is the real benefit of Continuously Improving—incremental improvements on a theme can be combined into meaningful achievements in your life.

It can feel daunting to try to constantly be improving all areas of our lives all the time. A significant benefit of the Level Up Method is that using it *reduces* overwhelm, one competency-strength combo at a time.

An effective approach to Continuously Improving is to focus on three aspects of your life that can yield big returns:

  1 your relationships with other people
  2 your relationship with time
  3 internal reflection

Continuously Improving in these three areas will yield a variety of advancements in other areas of your life.

When is the best time to initiate Continuously Improving? The answer may surprise you. The best time to begin making things better is when everything is going well. What? Think about it. When stuff needs to be done, or part of you needs to be fixed, you really have no choice but to attend to it. How you do so is up to you (competency-strength combos!), but what you do is not.

IMPROVE YOUR RELATIONSHIPS

In Chapter 9, we examined how to use our strengths when *Building* Collaborative Relationships. We now turn our attention to the importance of *maintaining* and *improving* those collaborative relationships.

When others depend upon you, you need your network more than ever. Strong mutual relationships give you a place to think aloud, share opinions, test ideas, and learn from mistakes—yours and others.

Relationships. Once you've got 'em, you have to work to keep 'em. Better to spend some effort improving your relationships than let them dissolve, only to have to replace them at some future date when they're needed. Like the song, "You don't know what you've got 'til it's gone."

Make a list of the important people in your life—above you, at your level, and at levels below yours—whom you do not regularly see at planned gatherings. Schedule some time to regularly keep in touch with each person. The frequency will be whatever you feel best serves the relationship—maybe biweekly, quarterly, or annually. If you can, touch base with them over the phone or in person, by email or text if you are unable to do so in real time.

Relationships are strengthened when both parties continue to bring something fresh to the table. Consider your strengths best suited to building relationships. Then contemplate which strengths could help you improve relationships. Bringing new strengths, and the perspectives that come with them, will help you keep your relationships stimulating. This works especially well with others who are also growing.

During any relationship, as one or both parties change, so too will the relationship. Bringing something into being is one thing, keeping it vital and durable is another.

PRACTICE TIME LEADERSHIP

The executive's time tends to belong to everybody else.
—Peter Drucker

Time is the new money.
—Richard Branson

Time, our most precious resource, is one we want to treat with care. We can either use our time wisely or waste it. Until someone invents a time machine, there will be no do-overs of the past. As for the present and the future, we've got you covered. Here you will learn not how to "spend" or "manage" your time, but how to use it more productively by *leading* it.

Time Leadership prevents unintentional overwhelm— accidentally trying to spin too many plates at once—and promotes a sense of control over your life. With time leadership, your productivity will soar, you will experience less schedule-related anxiety and stress, and you will be perceived as more in control of your life.

Work and personal life are now inextricably linked. No longer is there a work-life balance. Gone is the time for work and the time for self. Because we are now constantly accessible, we toggle back and forth between work and personal issues throughout our waking hours. We are always on. Rather than balance our work and our life, we now must integrate them into our daily schedules. Your outward-facing competencies will serve you well when meeting your commitments to others and accomplishing your goals. This inward-facing one can help you control a vital aspect of your life: your time.

Use Time Leadership to help you not just manage but *lead* your life.

> Q: What's better than time management?
> A: Time Leadership!

> Q: How do I lead my time?
> A: Simple. Assign each activity on your calendar a purpose and a competency-strength combo you will use to accomplish the purpose.

Q: What does that look like?

A: Here you go…

TIMEBOXING

Old idea, new name. Timeboxing is a technique to control your time and become more productive by scheduling your life in advance. In boxes. A proven time management tool, timeboxing is an effective way to avoid Parkinson's Law—"work expands to fill the time available." If you have observed this phenomenon in yourself or others, here is an effective and easy-to-remember approach to discourage it from happening in the future.

Time Leadership requires the addition of two things to each timebox:

- the *purpose* you hope to achieve during the time spent in this box
- one or more *competency-strength combos* you will use to achieve your purpose

Time Leadership takes a bit more thinking and planning at the front end and delivers a huge payoff at the back end.

Look at your calendar for next week. What do you see? Is it filled with cringeworthy obligatory appearances? Does it have some activities you are looking forward to? Are there open spaces? CEOs often have a lot of the first type on their calendars. For a vacation week, we want to see only the second and third kinds. Most of us have a variety of all three, plus several things we want to find time to attend to in the coming week.

First, the mandatories. They may be 1:1s, team meetings, or presentations. Say you have an informal meeting with a collaborator on an important project. The project is in its third week, scheduled for completion in six weeks. What purpose and competency-strength combos will you bring into this meeting? At this stage, you are looking for progress more than completion. So, your purpose might be twofold: to gain information and consider what will help each of you to get to the next step. Sounds obvious, but consider how much better this is than going into the meeting armed with only "What's up?" Consider using competency-strength combos that will facilitate your forward motion to the next milestone. How about Developing Plans-Achiever?

Also in the must-do category of calendar fillers might be a formal presentation to an audience important to you. Is your purpose to convey, convince, or both? Whichever it is, crafting your statements to be purpose driven will keep you on message. Now, which competency-strength combos will you use? Among the perennial favorites of effective presenters is the Inspiring Others-Communication combo.

When you see how Time Leadership can work for one type of activity in your life, you can apply it to others. The process for addressing each is the same: Assign a purpose and a competency-strength combo that might help you achieve it. Remember the saying, "When your only tool is a hammer, every problem looks like a nail"? Well, you've got *lots* of tools—all your competency-strength combos!

Warning: Although timeboxing can discourage the spontaneous appearance of Parkinson's Law—work expanding to fill the time available—it can have the opposite effect when you are scheduling your time. Nothing encourages Parkinson's Law to come in and pull up a chair like a welcoming void between two timeboxes. It is just begging to be filled with something, right? Wrong.

Cut yourself some slack. You don't have to schedule and competency-strength yourself to death. Leave some white spaces on the calendar.

If you must give the open spaces names, try:

- *Open Door.* Even if you don't have a door, just sit at your desk for a while and see what, or who, happens. Something, or someone, will.

- *Me Time.* Do something for you. Anything that feels like a time-out.

- *Walkabout.* Anywhere you choose. Walk, breathe, and look. Try to notice something new each time.

Time Leadership, timeboxing with a plan to make the most of your time, will give you a sense of control over your life.

In the next section, we will discuss a pleasant activity you will want to include on every week's calendar: reflection. But first, do you...

REMEMBER THE PETER PRINCIPLE?

The oft-quoted Peter Principle is an organizational concept developed by Laurence J. Peter. He observed that

people in a hierarchy tend to rise to their level of incompetence.

Think of occasions on which you have observed this phenomenon. What caused people to transit from competence at one level to incompetence at a higher one?

Was it because they didn't know which strengths to use in the new endeavor? Was it because they were using strengths that previously worked but were no longer the right ones? Or maybe their competencies were not the ones best suited to the new challenges? Or had they stopped Continuously Improving themselves?

Any one of these can cause leadership derailment.

Consider this photonegative of the Peter Principle, the Level Up Principle:

As they use their signature strengths to improve their competencies, and they continuously improve themselves, people in a hierarchy will rise to their highest achievable level of competence.

Problem solved.

MAKE TIME FOR INTENTIONAL REFLECTION

Reflecting is thinking about our attitudes and actions in the past, our goals and motives in the present, and how we might improve our approaches in the future. Include some time for regular reflection in your life.

A common tendency of high achievers is to treat themselves like a parent overscheduling their child. Busy, busy, busy all the time. Just as overscheduling your child is not a sign of good parenting, overscheduling yourself is not a sign of good Time Leadership.

This last section in our Continuously Improving competency gives encouragement to periodically hit the pause button in your life.

For a wonderful perspective on the benefit of reflection, this from Dov Seidman, CEO of LRN and one of the foremost experts in the study of behavior:[82]

> The most effective way to start is to pause. With a machine, hitting the pause button stops the action. But if you're a human being, that's when you start. You pause to make sense of your situation and to reconnect with your deepest beliefs. For business leaders, you pause to consider the fundamental issues that led your company down its current path and to its present challenges.

(Almost a century ago, in 1929, Coke's tagline was "The pause that refreshes.")

Plan some time for regular reflection, a combination of a time-out and me time. You don't have to share your reflections with anyone except your future self. One benefit of Reflection is the opportunity it provides for voluntary course correction. With pauses to reflect, you can anticipate the forks in the road before you suddenly come upon them at 70 mph.

Two activities that offer solid opportunities for self-development are practicing your new competency-strength combos and the time you spend in reflection—something most of us could do more of.

---

82 Dov Seidman, "Starting with a Pause," Strategy+Business newsletter, Oct 17, 2016.

Speaking of "more of," a terrific little exercise to include when reflecting is the activity called *more of, less of.* On your subject du jour, are there some things that it would be good to do *more* of? How about stuff you should do *less* of? Credit for best entry in this category goes to Marshall Goldsmith,[83] executive coach to mega-achievers:

> *Stop the annoying behavior and you'll stop*
> *being perceived as an annoyance.*

If there is one weakness we should work on, it is doing things that annoy others. And we know what those things are, right? Marshall exclaims, "It's so easy, I'm amazed I get paid to teach it!"

For competency-strength combos that can trigger ideas on how to do this, try pairing the Building Collaborative Relationships competency with any Interacting with Others strength.

When you are ready to attack your calendar, my question to you is this: Are you willing to invest 15 minutes each week to ensure your Continuous Improvement?

Great! Schedule a recurring time for reflection on each week's calendar. Try this:

---

83 Marshall Goldsmith, *What Got You Here Won't Get You There* (New York: Hachette Books, 2007).

Your Continuous Improvement Journal

2 min   Think about last week's entry. Rate your progress 1-10.

_____

_____

3 min   What will you try to get better at during the coming week?

_____

_____

_____

5 min   One thing you will do more of:

_____

_____

Which competency-strength combo will you try?

_____

_____

5 min   One thing you will do less of:

_____

_____

Which competency-strength combo will you try?

_____

_____

CONTINUALLY LEARNING AND IMPROVING—DO IT FOR YOU

Setting and achieving goals got you where you are today. You— we all—have a lot more to go. Here is a tip that will make the journey not only more pleasant but ultimately more effective: Be patient with yourself. Yes, the destination is important. But just being on the journey is more important. If you challenge yourself to make incremental progress, consciously work your competency-strength combos, and post results that are sustainable, give yourself credit for living a productive life.

Your competency-strength combos aren't just for reaching professional goals, they also come in handy in everyday life.

There's lots of talk these days about how employers engage their employees but, as Marshall Goldsmith observes, there's remarkably little about how employees engage *themselves*. The Level Up Method gives you a powerful tool, competency-strength combos, to deeply engage you in your work, your relationships, and your personal life.

To develop the whole you, consciously exercise your competency-strength combos to develop yourself in different directions. Select some topics about which you wish to acquire more knowledge or proficiency and do something about a few of them.

Maybe try one of these:

1 *Pick an academic subject you wish to know more about.*
   Read three books on it.
   Find a place in your life where you can use your new awareness.

How could you use your character strengths Curiosity, Love of Learning, or Appreciation of Beauty and Excellence?

How might your work strengths Discipline, Input, or Analytical be useful?

2 *Take a few lessons on an instrument.*
Play a verse or a tune for someone.
How might you use your character strengths Bravery, Perseverance, or Humor?
Will your work strengths Achiever, Arranger, or Self-Assurance be helpful?

3 *Prepare your garden for spring in a new way.*
See if it turns out to be what you had in mind.
Could your character strengths Bravery, Perseverance, or Humor help?
How about your work strengths Strategic, Arranger, or Achiever?

4 *Learn about an activity that would be fun for you and your children.*
Encourage everyone to get better each time they do it.
How could you use your character strengths Love, Teamwork, or Forgiveness?
How would you use your work strengths Includer, Developer, or Harmony?

5 *Train for a "fun run."*
Any distance you choose will be fine.
Could your character strengths Perseverance, Honesty or Self-Regulation help?
How would you use your work strengths Discipline, Self-Assurance, or Competition?

6 *Write and submit an article to your local paper.*
Bonus points if it is published. Either way, you did it.
Could your character strengths Creativity, Humility, or Prudence help?
How about your work strengths Strategic, Empathy, or Includer?

See? You can call upon your strengths to improve yourself in all kinds of ways!

Here are our last examples of how strengths can help us improve our competencies. Let's examine how two character strengths—Appreciation of Beauty and Excellence and Spirituality—and two work strengths—Discipline and Intellection—can help us as we are Continuously Improving.

CONTINUOUSLY IMPROVING WITH YOUR CHARACTER STRENGTHS

Appreciation of Beauty and Excellence®
Challenging ourselves to improve can take us a long way. There is so much to be done. But hard work can take us only so far. Beyond ourselves lies a whole other world that is ours to admire and aspire to, the world of beauty and excellence in others. Our

strength Appreciation of Beauty and Excellence is the doorway through which we can enter that world.

Use your strength Appreciation of Beauty and Excellence to help you continuously improve by aspiring to more deeply understand and admire exquisite and commendable examples of beauty, precision, uniqueness, achievements, and goodness. When you do, your sights will be lifted and your sense of what is possible will soar.

Homework assignment:
When those for whom you have special regard are feeling stuck, help them activate their own Appreciation of Beauty and Excellence. Consider a topic you know is of interest to them and do some research on new discoveries or examples related to it. Ask them if they have heard of this and if it would be an example of excellence that would be new and of interest to them. If it is, you will have helped them use their own Appreciation of Beauty and Excellence to get unstuck.

Spirituality®

Some strengths we can use to give ourselves a nice *push* to improve. The strengths of Appreciation of Beauty and Excellence and Spirituality are ones we can use to *pull* ourselves up a bit. Those with the strength Spirituality are not limited to improving themselves by what they can find in their own world. They know they are connected to something bigger than themselves and can draw upon it for clues and the inspiration to become better.

Use your Spirituality strength to continuously improve by pulling yourself toward your life's calling, toward your sacred beliefs of divinity, or toward your secular beliefs in humankind. Whatever the nature of your Spirituality strength, it will help you improve as you focus on a more personal and intimate relationship with that which lies beyond the range of human physical experience.

When you're feeling isolated, ask one with the Spirituality among her signature strengths to talk with you. Her beliefs that we are all connected to something greater may encourage you to consider how not alone you are in the world.

CONTINUOUSLY IMPROVING WITH YOUR WORK STRENGTHS

Discipline®

Discipline, the strength without a snooze button on top of its alarm clock, is a nice one to have when we are Continuously Improving. After all, "delayed improving" is not what we're after. Discipline is the man with a plan. Discipline likes routine, structure, and doing its part. What is the biggest obstacle most of us face when trying to improve? Getting started, right? Discipline *loves* showing up on time.

When you want to get serious about developing yourself, engage Discipline to assist you. Discipline, a master at creating organized frameworks, can help you structure your life in a way that optimizes your relationships, makes productive use of your time, and includes periodic reflection. What to do if you don't have Discipline among your signature strengths? Consider which strengths you do have that could be combined to provide what Discipline would bring to developing yourself. Maybe a combination of some Deliberative, Responsibility, Consistency, Arranger, and Achiever? That works.

Intellection®

Intellection, a strength in our Thinking Thoroughly set, may not seem an obvious candidate to support our Continuous Learning. But Intellection, with its capacity for quiet reflection and consideration, is a great strength to help us determine the *direction* of our self-improvement.

We all know people who overschedule themselves and, as a result, produce a lot of busyness. It seems like their work *and* their play are always expanding to fill the time available (thanks again, Mr. Parkinson). Unrestrained, they may self-induce "hurry sickness," the stress and anxiety that result from continual feelings of urgency.

Engage Intellection to put the brakes on that nonsense. What does Intellection do? Intellection *thinks carefully* before initiating action. If you could benefit from better planning and course correcting to help you be Continuously Improving, engage Intellection to help you think things through.

When you allow Intellection to consider the alternatives and how they might fit together, you may get some *aha!* moments, those little discoveries we make that charge our enthusiasm to get underway. Thanks, Intellection, we needed that.

PART III

Your Goals

They Give You a Sense of Purpose

You cannot expect to achieve new goals or move beyond your present circumstances unless you change.
—Les Brown

The beginning is always today.
—Mary Shelley

Our goals are results we wish to achieve. Goals may be in service to ourselves, to others, or to an organization we belong to or support.

While organizational goals are "shared" among team members and propel individuals and the organization toward the vision for itself, your personal goals pull *you* toward your desired vision for *yourself.* Your objectives in life are the specific achievements that will help you reach each of your goals.

VISION←GOALS←OBJECTIVES

Our goals connect us to what lies ahead in our lives.

With goals, we can think in the future and act in the present, one objective at a time.

We often hear about how to motivate others. If only. The only ones who can motivate us are ourselves. Other people may not be able to motivate us, but there are three classes of things that can and do motivate us—our vision, our values, and our goals.

Let's see how all three of these come together when we set goals for ourselves.

GOAL SETTING

Your Connection to Forward Motion

Whether you think you can or you can't, you're right.
—Henry Ford

Equipped now with your signature strengths and an understanding of how you can use them to develop competencies, you are ready to set some goals of your own.

Why do we set goals? Because setting goals encourages our forward motion toward our vision. Setting goals also brings a sense of *purpose* to our lives.

Accomplishing our goals, what the Level Up Method is designed to help us do, gives our lives *meaning*. Like this:

PAST ACCOMPLISHMENTS		DESIRED FUTURE
& EXPERIENCES		& VISION
	→PRESENT STATE→	
MEANING		PURPOSE

Think of each of your goals as a three-legged stool, supported by your vision, your values, and your strengths. With each of these sturdy legs, your goals will have firm support. Remove one or more of the legs—vision, values, or strengths—and the stool, your goal, loses some of its stability and will not serve its purpose. But with each firmly in place, your goals will be solid.

This is the BIG IDEA of Part III:

Use your vision, your values, and your strengths to determine the best goals for you.

Your
VISION
for Yourself in the Future

+

Your
VALUES

+

Your Signature
STRENGTHS

=

Your
GOALS
for Yourself in the Present

Let's take them one at a time.

YOUR VISION

Your vision is the mental image of what you can and want to be.

The first step in setting a goal is to bring into focus the desirable visions you have for your future self at specific times.

Start by sketching out the advanced long-term version of you, say in five to ten years. Write down a few descriptors that capture it. Your advanced vision will want to be more obtainable than eternal peace and happiness. That would be Nirvana, a vision that has proved elusive for 25 centuries. For a few examples of vision statements from exemplary people and organizations, see those in Chapter 7 under Creating Vision. Note that each is brief and clearly stated, as yours will be.

Then, consider what you would like the next version of you to be, say in one to three years. This will be the working version of your vision, the one that will guide you when setting your near-term goals.

As a high achiever, you are already *good*. The next version of you will be *better*, and the advanced version will be you at your *best*. Good, better, best. That's your journey.

Take a screenshot of the person you want to be next. What do you see...what details do you notice? Dream, but be practical. For your vision, include a few of the capabilities and accomplishments of the next, better version of you. Capture this vision of yourself in a paragraph or two. Put it where you can find it when you need it for inspiration or direction.

YOUR VALUES

Our values are the qualities most important to us. They motivate how we think and act. They serve as the standards to which we hold ourselves accountable. Living your values is always a good idea.

> *This above all: to thine own self be true.*
> —William Shakespeare, *Hamlet*

Over time, our vision will evolve. But our values and strengths will remain stable. Ever wonder why someone acts the way he does? If you can know his values, you may have the answer. Values drive a big part of how we think and act.

Whether you are choosing values for yourself or an organization, select those that align with the most cherished beliefs. In organizations, aligning values, strategy, and culture is a big deal. For the last list of potential values that you will ever need, see our Level Up Large List of Values in Appendix B, 400 of them for your consideration. Select the three to five that best represent what is most important to you. The words for our values may be common and simple. However, the way we embrace and reflect our values can be very uncommon and anything but simple. A few sample values: Nelson Mandela, Equality; Tom Brady, Commitment; Zappos, Service; Abraham Lincoln, Honesty; L.L. Bean, Integrity; Bill & Melinda Gates Foundation, Optimism; Albert Einstein, Truth. (If you would like to know what my values are, you can find them in the Help with Your Journey section at the end of the book.)

What are yours?

YOUR STRENGTHS

You already know all about strengths. This placeholder is just a reminder to consider your signature strengths in your goal-setting process. Remember that your signature strengths will play significant roles in setting your goals. Your intermediate strengths are waiting in the wings to be summoned when you need them. Taken together, you likely have 40 to 45 signature and intermediate strengths to draw upon when achieving whatever goals you set for yourself.

Which of your signature strengths will you use to live your values on the way to realizing your vision?

SET SMART GOALS

When setting your goals and forming your objectives, consider using the SMART way to ensure they will get you to the result you wish to achieve.[84] Use this tool to stimulate and expand your thinking on something you want to accomplish. As you consider a goal or an objective, ask:

- Is it a **S**pecific improvement?
- Is it **M**easurable?
- Is it **A**chievable in the time allowed?
- Is the goal **R**ealistic, given available resources?
- Can it be done on **T**ime?

SMART is a handy tool to advance your thinking on each goal and objective you are considering.

---

84 George T. Doran, "There's a S.M.A.R.T. Way to Write Management's Goals and Objectives," *Management Review*, November 1981.

5 TIPS ON GOAL SETTING

Tip #1. Only set goals you truly want to accomplish,
ones that motivate you. Each goal needs your own personal
"why" behind it. Frequently mentioned reasons for setting goals:

- Self-improvement: knowledge, accomplishments, or improved capabilities

- Meeting a challenge or seizing an opportunity to do something for yourself or another

- Money or possessions

Knowing your why makes it easier to create a clear goal and commit to it.

Focus on the projects that matter. Spend your time and energies on high-potential projects and with high-potential people. Support and develop them with your competency-strength combos. Give yourself permission to cease doing things that are not moving you toward your vision of yourself. Consider what you need to do more of and what you could do less of.

Tip #2. The simple act of setting a goal puts you in a positive place.
When you set a goal, you favorably impact your ability to achieve it. Setting goals makes them appear more vivid and attainable sooner.

Sapere Vedere
(Believing is Seeing)
—Leonardo da Vinci

Pronounced "sah-PARE-ay veh-DARE-ay," this was da Vinci's motto. He transposed "seeing is believing" to "believing is seeing." A master of using vision as a positive force to propel his accomplishments, he embraced the concept that if you *believe* you can do it, you will be able to *see* yourself doing it. How powerful is that!

This is closely related to another visioning concept from Leonardo:

> "There are three types of people:
>> those who see,
>> those who see when they are shown,
>> those who do not see."

Work on seeing and believing what others cannot; include what you can see and believe in your vision. Do this and, when it comes time to set your goals, you will be way ahead of the pack.

Tip #3. Accomplishing even a small goal yields big benefits.
Give yourself opportunities for early wins. Nothing provides momentum and hope like achieving something. Start with Goldilocks goals: not too hard, but not too easy.

Use the Level Up Method to generate small wins early. Every time you use a competency-strength combination to get something done, you experience a little win, causing your brain to release some dopamine, the feel-good neurotransmitter.

This jumpstarts your productivity and encourages you to repeat the experience.

When you repeat the process to achieve other small wins, your brain will store what you accomplished and how you did it. When you find yourself facing a similar challenge, you will be able to retrieve the competency-strength combo that worked, replicate the effort, and enjoy another successful result.

Fortunately, or not, our brains learn better from successes than failures.

Imagine you are running a relay race. A clean baton change takes about as much time as the blink of an eye. If you drop the baton, what do you learn? If you did not know what you were doing, the answer is probably nothing. But if you study the proper technique and can match your stride, arm and hand movements, and signals with those of the other runner, you will make a little progress each time you attempt the handoff. You may not learn much from your mistakes, but you will learn a lot from your successes—the incremental improvements you make each time you attempt to do something a bit better. Eventually, everything will fall into place and you will succeed. Practice it a few more times immediately and you will own it. As the athlete draws upon athletic competency-strength combos that have helped him achieve his objectives, you can use the ones in Level Up to accomplish yours. And remember how you did so for use another time.

Then you will be ready to try a new competency-strength combination to produce another small but different kind of win. The result will be a little more dopamine, encouragement to keep going, and new memories of success in different endeavors.

Tip #4. Simplify.

Consider as many potential goals as you wish. But dedicate yourself to no more than three important ones at any time. Apply most of your focus to the most important goal and try to accomplish it in as few steps as possible.

For an amazing example of simplifying the incomprehensible, consider NASA's mission to land a man on the moon and safely return him. The challenge was issued in 1961 by JFK.

This was going to be an incredibly complex task. But rather than starting with the complicated, they went the other direction, toward simplification, and asked "To win this war, what is the fewest number of battles we need to win?"

They used this narrowing process to arrive at:

Propulsion, Navigation, Life Support

There is no comparison, really, between the challenges NASA faced at that time and the ones we deal with in our lives (unless we are Elon Musk or Jeff Bezos). Still, fewer is usually better. The fewer clubs you need to get around the golf course, the fewer steps from your bed to the bathroom, the fewer miles in your commute, and the fewer people you must please. Likewise, the fewer goals it takes us to achieve our vision and the fewer competency-strength combos we must call upon to reach them, the more likely we are to succeed. Just like a machine, fewer moving parts = less potential for breakdown.

Employ the Level Up Method as if you are on a critical path. The critical path is the fewest number of steps necessary to achieve a certain result. Simplify. Reduce the steps between you and your goal.

Tip #5. Take it easy on yourself.
When we buckle down in the present and give it everything we've got for a payoff in the future, those little voices of self-doubt can transform our enthusiasm into uncertainty. Some of this is natural, helpful really. But there is no reason to let concern advance to worry and worry to anxiety. A leading cause of anxiety is trying to be perfect.

> *No one is "perfect." Yet many people struggle to be perfectionists, which can trigger a cascade of anxieties.*[85]

You already have enough stress in your life. Use the Level Up Method to lessen it, not add to it. This is not one of those things where you must give 110 percent. The building is not on fire. Set your energy level on this at 80 percent. You're in it for the long haul. Your goal is not to be perfect, just to be better.

The Level Up Method was created to provide you a natural way to make every next step on your journey a productive one. You're not working with some else's systems and parts to reach *their* goals. Everything you are using is all yours—your values, your strengths, your goals, and your competencies. Seth Godin calls anxiety the act of "experiencing failure in advance." Using the Level Up Method, you prevent this and experience the opposite—success in the present. You don't need the concentration of a jeweler to make this work for you. As long as you approach it with your intention and commitment, you will be fine.

---

85 Dr. Jeff Szymanski, *Anxiety and Stress Disorders,* Harvard Medical School Journal, January 2019.

A LAYERED APPROACH TO GOAL SETTING

Not all goals and not all competency-strength combos are created equal. Some will be more valuable to you than others. To achieve the results you desire, use your most potent competency-strength combos where they will have their greatest impact.

Consider your efforts to improve as you would the layers and blocks in a pyramid.

VISION

GOAL   GOAL   GOAL

PRIMARY OBJECTIVES
for one of the goals

Objective   Objective   Objective
Competency-Strength   *Competency-Strength*   *Competency-Strength*

SECONDARY OBJECTIVES
for one of a goal's primary objectives

Objective   Objective   Objective
Competency-Strength   *Competency-Strength*   *Competency-Strength*

When we think of a pyramid, its most significant feature, aside from the sheer mass of the thing, is probably the point at the top. But when we build a pyramid, we begin at the base. It's no different with your goals and objectives. First, consider how high you want to go. These are your goals. Next, design the structure necessary to support the effort to get there. These are your objectives. Then, get to work laying those blocks at the bottom, one at a time. The two most tangible goals when building a pyramid are to provide a safe place for something that is considered sacred or valuable and to support the pointy top at its place in the sky. The uppermost intangible goal may be to send a powerful message.

Thinking: Top Down
Picture yourself achieving your intermediate vision, becoming the person you want to be in one to three years. What goals will you have to accomplish to achieve this? If NASA could get to the moon with three goals, propulsion, navigation, and life support, we should also be able to work effectively on reaching our vision with three goals. Clearly state each one, and check that it can be a SMART goal for you.

Now, break each goal into three objectives you will have to accomplish in order to reach your goal. These will be your primary objectives. Each of your primary objectives will be supported by secondary objectives.

Let's walk through two examples of what this might look like. Say you want to launch an initiative to provide a new product to the customers of your business *and* you wish to remodel your kitchen at home. Yes, you have a full life!

Here are simplified and condensed models of how you might set the goals and objectives for each:

For your business goal:

Launch an initiative to provide a fresh and original product to your customers, one that will be valuable to them in new ways and will draw upon your existing production and marketing capabilities.

Your primary objectives may be product, people, place.

  1   Create a product that is desirable and producible.
  2   Get the right people on board.
  3   Secure a place for the work to be done.

The secondary objectives for getting the right people on board may be:

  1   Create the job descriptions for those who will be needed.
  2   Select and hire the best for each role.
  3   Indoctrinate, train, and engage the new team members.

For your home goal:

Plan a new kitchen where you can gather with your family or friends to prepare a meal and enjoy the evening together.

Your primary objectives might be attractive, functional, affordable.

1   Describe an environment that is attractive.

2   Design it to be functional.

3   Choose an approach that is affordable.

The secondary objectives for describing an environment that is attractive might be:

1   Identify the look and feel you want.

2   Find and hire the most suitable kitchen designer.

3   Integrate the kitchen design with the rest of the home.

The final step of Thinking: Top Down is to consider which competency-strength combinations you will use to accomplish each primary objective and each secondary objective.

For instance:

Example 1

For your business goal, one of your primary objectives is to get the right people on board. A secondary objective of getting the right people is to:

■   Indoctrinate, train, and engage the new team members.

One useful competency-strength combo to use when carrying out these secondary objectives might be:

■   Inspiring Others-Communication.

Example 2

For your home goal, one of your primary objectives is to describe a kitchen that is attractive. A supporting, secondary objective is to:

- Find and hire the most suitable kitchen designer.

A useful competency-strength combo to use when hiring the designer might be:

- Building Collaborative Relationships-Appreciation of Beauty and Excellence.

When you consider in advance which competency-strength combos you might use to accomplish your objectives, you will accelerate any goal or project from the inside out. You will be able to get traction on your goal quickly and make smoother transitions from one objective to another.

Doing: Bottom Up
Start at the bottom with the secondary objectives for one of your goals. As you work on these first with preselected competency-strength combos, you will quickly generate momentum toward your goal. When you've accomplished all the secondary objectives for one of the primary objectives, you can move your focus to another primary objective.

For instance, in a perfect world:[86]

As you put together the job descriptions for those who will be needed to produce the new product, you can select and hire the best for each role. When you have indoctrinated, trained, and engaged your new team members, you will have achieved your objective—to get the right people on board. Or you will be very close to it.

Prescient planners (lucky them) often find that completing the final secondary objective is also the last step in meeting the primary objective. The rest of us usually need to revisit what we have accomplished versus what we wanted to achieve. We may wish to add another secondary objective or two before we can put a bow on the primary objective and call it done.

Whatever efforts you expend and whatever results you produce along the way, remember Goal Setting Tip #5: Take it easy on yourself. It is natural to occasionally become so immersed in meeting specific targets that we temporarily become forgetful of the big picture, the vision we are trying to achieve. We know we should set SMART goals, but we want to keep in mind that the *goal* is the goal, not the *measurement* of the goal.

An excellent article on this in *Harvard Business Review*[87] reminds us that often "metrics are flawed proxies for what you care about." So yes, let's set goals that are measurable, but let's measure what *matters* and not let the measurement of a SMART goal hijack its other equally important features.

---

86 Term for an imaginary place. "Strive for excellence, not perfection, because we don't live in a perfect world." —Joyce Meyer
87 Michael Harris and Bill Tayler, "Don't Let Metrics Undermine Your Business," *Harvard Business Review*, October 2019.

Coming up in Chapter 13, 7 Steps to Level Up, you will have an opportunity to use this layered approach when you create your own goals and objectives using the Level Up framework.

LESS IS MORE AND MORE IS MORE

The fewer competency-strength combos you must use to get something done, the fewer moving parts of your working plan, the more focused and efficient your efforts will be.

But when it comes to the total number of competency-strength combos you have, more is better. The proven ones, where the competency and the strength have been woven together, make up your Constellation of Competencies. We can't have too many of these.

The more woven competency-strength combos you have, the quicker you will be able to find the best solution to a problem. As you learn to use your unique combos, you will find your efforts become less erratic. Your attempts will begin to yield more desirable outcomes and help you perform in a more productive and predictable manner. As you become more consistent at hitting your targets, others will wonder "how'd he *do* that?"

Occasionally, take some shots that are a stretch for you. When you know doing so isn't going to cause any collateral damage, go for it. That's how you grow. The results may surprise you.

Twenty years from now you will be more disappointed
by the things you didn't do than by the ones you did do.
So throw off the bowlines. Sail away from
the safe harbor. Catch the trade winds in your sails.
Explore. Dream. Discover.
—Mark Twain

WE'RE GETTING CLOSER

You are now prepared to use the Level Up concepts to take yourself on a journey. Your destination: the next better version of yourself. As you do so, you will step out of your comfort zone. To achieve the accomplishments you desire, you will have to do some things differently. It will take a while to get used to your new habits. Some uneasiness is natural when consciously improving performance in any field. Remember,

Growth and comfort cannot co-exist.

You can either step forward into growth, or backwards into security.
—Abraham Maslow

It won't be easy. Neither will it be terribly hard; 80 percent effort will be plenty.

You come to this fully prepared to succeed. You have all the tools and will set for yourself goals you are fully capable of achieving. The only other provisions you will need on your journey are your intention to commence the process and your commitment to see it through. As you begin to develop your talents into strengths and direct your competencies toward your goals, you will have

305

the sensation that you are moving. You will become unstuck! You will become more optimistic and enthusiastic. And your self-belief will soar.

One of the most important factors about becoming successful is self-belief. In other words, your opinion of how successful you will be is generally accurate.[88]

If you *think* it will work, it *will* work.

Coming up, in Chapter 12, we will peek behind the curtains of

- the *Level Up Method*, potent competency-strength combos to help you achieve any goal

- the *7 Steps to Level Up*, your personal development program to become the best possible version of you

As we do so, you will gain a deeper understanding of the powerful concepts underpinning them: the scientific method and Intentional Change Theory.

Then, in Chapter 13, we will take you through each of the 7 Steps to Level Up as you consider how to select and launch the first project to get you on your way.

---

88 Anthony Moore, "14 Principles You Must Master to Become Successful," Mission.org, August 10, 2017.

CHAPTER 12

On the Shoulders of Giants

Credit is Due

THE LEVEL UP METHOD AND FRAMEWORK IN CONTEXT

A framework is a structure that gives us a place for a process to occur. It provides the spaces in which we will do things with our tools, practices, and methods. Our 7 Steps to Level Up is an example of a framework.

A *methodology* is a set of tools and activities to solve a specific problem with an approach that is repeatable. The Level Up Method is an example of one.

A *system* is a collection of things that work together in an interconnected way.

Together, the Level Up Method and the 7 Steps to Level Up are your Level Up System.

In the next chapter, you will be introduced to the *7 Steps to Level Up*. You can use this framework as the process to develop the best possible version of you. The key ingredient of the framework is the *Level Up Method*, which consists in engaging your signature strengths to support the competencies that will help you achieve your objectives. Use the Level Up Method, the 7 Steps to Level Up, and what already works well in your life to create your personal Level Up System for success.

Have you ever heard of the mantra of the consultant: frameworks, tools, solutions? A very effective problem-solving tool, it summarizes the best way to address any complex issue in just three words. We use this approach to create the *Level Up System*:

Framework	The 7 Steps to Level Up
Tools	The Level Up Method, your competency-strength combos
Solutions	Level Up to the next better version of you

When you are working on a project to take you closer to your vision, the framework, tools, solutions model can help you plan and organize it in an effective way.

When Isaac Newton wrote in 1676,

If I have seen further, it is by standing on the shoulders of giants,

he was recognizing the contributions that others' accomplishments made to his own discoveries.[89] Similarly, our Level Up Method and 7 Steps to Level Up framework owe debts of gratitude to the influence of two benchmark predecessors, the scientific method and Intentional Change Theory.

Let's review each and see how we benefit from it.

---

89 Newton's version was a resurrection of the concept's earlier mention by Bernard, chancellor of the cathedral school of Chartres c. 1120 AD, *nanos gigantum humeris insidentes*, we are like dwarves perched on the shoulders of giants.

*The Scientific Method
and the Level Up Method*

The scientific method, which consists of learning through observation, has guided thoughtful inquiry since the 17th century. For it, we have Sir Francis Bacon to thank.[90]

You were probably first exposed to the scientific method when you were a child. The next time you see an elementary school field trip at a museum, zoo, or live presentation, listen in on how the teacher is engaging the class. You will probably hear the words "see," "think," and "wonder." "Class, what did we *see* today? What do you *think* about that? What does it make you *wonder*?" When the kids answer, you can hear their wheels turning. Getting the little ones to wonder begins their journey of learning by trying new ways of thinking and doing things. This is the basis of the scientific method.

Fast forward to adulthood. Unless we are involved in scientific inquiry, we probably use the scientific method to address issues in our lives without giving it much thought. After 500 years of translation, there are several versions of it. Most have five to eight steps. Here's one with six steps:

1 Make an observation
2 Ask a question
3 Form a hypothesis
4 Experiment
5 Note the results
6 Draw a conclusion

90 Another discovery made "on the shoulders of giants": In 1621, Bacon published *Novum Organum Scientiarum*. His "new scientific method" replaced the original Organon, written by Aristotle in 350 BC.

For maximum effectiveness, use the *Level Up Method* within the broader context of the scientific method. Here's how:

To make progress toward a	*Accomplish an*	*by improving a*	*that is supported by a*
Goal	←Objective	←Competency	←Strength

If you want to get better at something, develop and test your competency-strength combos using the steps of the scientific method:

1	Observation	I would like to be perceived as more of a leader, but I'm not as effective in meetings as I would like to be.
2	Question	Which competency could I support with one of my signature strengths to demonstrate my leadership capability?
3	Hypothesis	A competency useful to leaders is Influencing Others. I would like to be more influential. Among my signature strengths is Self-Assurance. I do feel self-assured, but I do not always project confidence when I am in groups. To help others understand and appreciate my point of view, in the next team meeting I will try to project more of the confidence I feel.

4   Experiment   In the meeting, I gave freer rein to my Self-Assurance to express an opinion on an issue important to me that the group was considering.

5   Results   When I demonstrated more of the confidence that I felt, the result was contagious. Others came to agree with my perspective. My Self-Assurance helped me Influence Others.

6   Conclusion   I see that people respect Self-Assurance in others and are more influenced by people who act with confidence.
I believe I have made progress toward my objective to be more influential. For confirmation, I will ask someone whose opinion I respect if they noted any change in my behavior in the meeting, and how they thought it was received by the others. This information will help me think about using more of my Self-Assurance or another strength to improve my emerging Influencing Others competency.

The steps of the scientific method can help you to objectify the results of applying competency-strength combos in specific situations and increase your ability to move toward your objectives and goals.

Intentional Change Theory
and the 7 Steps to Level Up

Intentional Change Theory is an excellent five-step model to describe the progress of self-directed learning. It was developed by Dr. Richard Boyatzis of Case Western Reserve University.[91] Dr. Boyatzis examined how people made changes to their behavior and captured the patterns he found in his "five discoveries," a cycle that repeats as a person changes:

1 The ideal self and a personal vision
2 The real self and its comparison to the ideal self
3 A learning agenda and plan
4 Experimentation with the new behaviors, thoughts, and perceptions
5 Develop and maintain relationships to support each discovery in the process

Dr. Boyatzis and his colleagues have spent 50 years studying what it takes to create lasting change. Many self-improvement and self-development plans, including ours, have benefitted from his findings. Intentional Change Theory's five stages and Level Up's seven steps, which you will see in the next chapter, are both useful ways to shrink the Gap, that place between who you are now and your ideal, achievable vision for yourself. To do so, Level Up introduces competency-strength combos as tools you can use to achieve your goals.

---

91 R. E. Boyatzis, "The Five Stages of Intentional Change Theory," Key Step Media, February 21, 2017.

HOW IT ALL WORKS, A PREVIEW

One way to think of these concepts:

The
7 Steps to Level Up
provides a unique way to apply
Intentional Change Theory
to move toward your vision of the best possible version of
yourself.

A key feature in the framework of the
7 Steps to Level Up
is the
Level Up Method,
pulling competencies supported by strengths toward your goals.
You can use
the scientific method
to create and test competency-strength combos to achieve your
goals and objectives.

Taken together, *the Level Up Method* and *7 Step framework*
comprise *the*
Level Up System.

As you use it, you will
Level Up!

Now, let's put it all together in one place where you can use
everything you've got to get where you want to go. Up next, your
7 Steps to Level Up.

CHAPTER 13

7 Steps to Level Up

Your Personal Development Plan

*The Level Up Framework:
a process to help you be the best possible version of you*

Nothing is particularly hard if you divide it up into small jobs.
—Henry Ford

*For the things we have to learn before we can do them, we learn by
doing them.*
—Aristotle

Nobody gets better automatically. There must be a plan.
When we are in school, the curriculum is the plan. When
we join the workforce, the organization may offer training to
help us succeed at *their* plan. We need our own plan. That's what
this is—your plan.

When you have a plan, you give structure to the process of your
self-development. You decide what is important to you, what
you want to achieve, and how you will accomplish it.

With the 7 Steps as your personal development plan, you will
productively apply your potent competency-strength combos
in a framework that will enable you to become the next better

version of you. You will score small wins early, making headway on the shift you want to achieve. Every time you take a small step forward, it will brighten your outlook and give you a sense of more forward momentum.

It's all here for you: the framework, the methodology, the tools, and the techniques most likely to help you produce the kinds of results that will move you closer to your vision of the next version of you.

With the 7 Steps as your companion and guide on your journey, you will use your unique competency-strength combos to pursue opportunities in original and powerful ways and upgrade the current version of you. And the next time you get stuck, you can use this process to free yourself.

Earlier, we said a key feature in the 7 Steps is the Level Up Method. Can you guess what the *central feature* of the 7 Steps is? Right, it's *you!* The work, and it is work, of moving through any process in an effort to improve ourselves is easy to talk about, but—you already know this—can be hard to do. However, if you are motivated and don't skip over or rush any steps, you will be able to produce some durable results for yourself. If you find the process challenging and humbling, you know you're doing it right.

7 STEPS TO LEVEL UP

1   *Vision*

Create a desirable and achievable vision of the next version of you, the person you want to be personally and professionally in one to three years. Include the values you will live and the signature strengths you will more fully engage.

2   *The Gap*

Assess the Gap between your vision and where you are now. Consider what improvements will move you toward your vision.

3   *Goals*

Identify three goals to reduce the Gap between the current and the future you. Select goals that exemplify your values and make good use of your strengths. Place them in the order in which you will work on them.

4   *Objectives*

Start with the goal you wish to achieve first. Break it down into three primary objectives that will help you reach it. Place them in the order in which you will work on them. Assign to each primary objective a few secondary objectives that will help you accomplish it. Repeat the process for each goal and primary objective.

5   *Competency-Strength Combinations*

For each objective, select a competency that will enable you to achieve it. Then choose one of your signature character or work strengths that will bring the competency to life. Repeat for each of your primary and secondary objectives.

6   *Practice*
Begin with the easiest secondary objective of the primary objective you wish to accomplish first. Try using the most logical competency-strength combo on the objective. If it helped you achieve the objective, great. If not, try others until you get your first small win.

7   *Assess*
Review the results of each effort. Consider what worked and what didn't. Use your new information to revise any plans made earlier in Steps 3–5.

8. There is no Step 8. But if there were a Step 8, it would be… Repeat!

The BIG IDEA of 7 Steps to Level Up:

Begin with goals that embrace your vision, values, and strengths. Use your competency-strength combinations to accomplish them and you *will* Level Up.

Your
VISION,
VALUES & STRENGTHS

+

GOALS & OBJECTIVES

+

COMPETENCY-STRENGTH COMBOS
The Level Up Method

+

PRACTICE

=

LEVEL UP!
The Next Better Version of You

A few things to think about along the way:

1   *Your Vision*

Picture what excellence will look like for you. Create a long-term vision for yourself, the person you would like to be in five to ten years. This will be the *advanced* version of you. Write down a few descriptors that capture it in one phrase or sentence. For some exemplary long-term vision statements, see those in Chapter 7, under Creating Vision.

Now, create the vision that captures the *next* version of you, the person you want to be in one to three years. This will be the working version of your vision, the one that will guide you when setting your goals. See if you can capture it in a paragraph. As a high achiever, you are already *good*. The next version of you will be *better,* and the advanced version will be you at your *best*. Good, better, best. That's your journey.

2   *The Gap*
Use the illustration of the Gap to visualize what you need to do and when you will need to do it to reduce the distance between the current you and the ideal you.

You can -

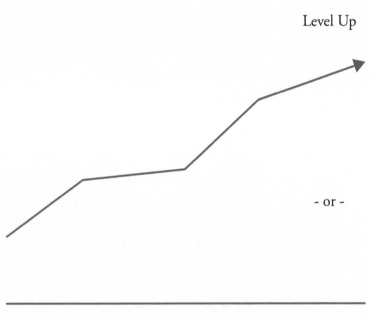

Level Up

- or -

Do nothing

Have you ever been told to think outside the box? Annoying, wasn't it? Most of what is outside the box is *impossible*. A more useful, and agreeable, concept is "think *inside* the Gap." Use the mental picture of the Gap you want to fill to focus on what is *possible.*

Ways to think *in* the Gap:
    Where do I want to go?
    When do I want to arrive?
    Where am I now?
    What do I need to improve?
    What can I achieve first to get underway?

3   *Your Goals*

List the accomplishments that can help you shorten the distance between you and your vision.

Use the Eisenhower Matrix to determine your best candidates—those that are Important but Not Urgent.

State each accomplishment in terms of a goal. For example,

Accomplishment	Advance my knowledge about my profession
Goal	Attend a training program to become certified in *x*; or engage in a program of self-study by doing *y*

From your list, choose the three goals that can play the biggest roles in your advancement. One way to select them:

Identify one that will seize or create opportunities, one that will minimize a threat to your advancement, and one that will help you develop yourself personally. This 1-1-1 mix is a good way to begin thinking about your goals and what they can do for you. Or you can revise the 1-1-1 mix to whatever best serves your vision.

Check each one to qualify it as a SMART goal.
Is the goal
    Specific?
    Measurable?
    Achievable?
    Realistic?
    Timely?

Write a brief description of each goal and the benefit that achieving it will bring. For reference, see 5 Tips on Goal Setting in Part III: Your Goals.

Place your three goals in the order in which you will work on them.

4   *The objectives for your goals*
If you have three goals with three primary objectives each and three secondary objectives for each primary objective, you will have found 39 new ways to improve! Take your time to complete this step. Somewhere between three days and two weeks should do it. When it is good enough—it doesn't have to be perfect—you will know it. How will you know? When you become eager to get

started working on some of your new objectives, the 1.0 version of your goals and objectives is ready for action.

One way to write your objectives is in terms of what you want more of or what you want less of.

Most of your objectives will be about positioning you closer to ideas, possessions, activities, or people you want *more of* in your life. But some will be about things or people you want *less of* in your life. Insightful observation from Michael Bungay Stanier, "The desire for change is often driven by the need to get away from what is *not* working for us."[92]

Stating an objective in these terms will add clarity to your understanding of what you need to do to achieve it.

5   *Competency-strength combos*
Creating the competency-strength combos that will help you achieve your objectives is the Level Up Method:

To make progress Accomplish an by engaging a that is supported by a toward a

Goal←Objective←Competency←Strength

Creating competency-strength combos to achieve your goals and objectives is your *strategy*.

Are you thinking that there are a lot of competency-strength combos from which to choose? There are

92 Michael Bungay Stanier, "The Five Question Leader," WBECS Summit webinar, November 29, 2018.

indeed—58 strengths and 17 competencies make for 986 different competency-strength combinations to address any goal or objective.

The 986 combos are available to all of us but not to each of us. Consider: If your signature strengths are those in the top quartile of your character and work strengths, you would have 15 signature strengths. 15 x 17 = 255 potential competency-strength combos from which to choose. That should be enough for you to get any job done.

Think of achieving each objective with a competency-strength combo as you would a safe with a combination lock that requires only two numbers to open. The first number, the competency, is between 1 and 17. The second number, the signature strength you will apply, is between 1 and 15. If there was something you really wanted in a safe and you were down to your last 255 combinations, would you try them? Of course you would. Two turns of the dial and, eventually, open sesame!

For a general approach to help you find the right combo to try first, select the competency *category* and the strength *set* that feel like logical starting places. Using the diagram below, begin by focusing on just one of the 25 squares. Consider which of your combos in this square might work. Nothing here? How about another square, one with the same category of competency but a different set of strength? Continue until you select a combo that feels like it might work.

In our competency-strength grid, the sets of strengths are the vertical columns and the categories of competencies are the horizontal rows:

Competency-Strength Grid

Use your **Strengths**	to improve your **Competencies**				
	THINK STRATEGICALLY	LEAD PEOPLE	LEAD CHANGE	DRIVE RESULTS	DEVELOP SENSE
STRATEGIC THINKING	X	X	X	X	X
RELATIONSHIP BUILDING	X	X	X	X	X
INFLUENCING	X	X	X	X	X
EXECUTING	X	X	X	X	X

6   *Practice*

Want to know the powerful secret to using your strengths to improve your competencies? It's *practice*.

That's it. If you practice them, they will come. If you don't? Well, you know…

As Gary Player said, "The more I practice, the luckier I get."

As you practice, you further develop your signature strengths and expand your Constellation of Competencies.

Practice using your competency-strength combos to rehearse your future and decrease the distance between you and your goals.

Do the work. Address your goals one objective and one competency-strength combo at a time.

Each time you engage a competency-strength combo to work on an objective, you are using one of your *tactics*, or tools to execute your strategy in pursuit of your objective.

You can jumpstart any project by working with a challenge that can be met quickly. Same here. Go for a small win early and begin making progress by engaging with the easiest objective of the goal you wish to achieve first.

7   *Assess results*
Are you getting closer to meeting your objective?

If you achieved your objective with the first combo, pick another objective and cycle back to step five. If the combo was effective but there is still more to be done on the objective, pick another combo and try to do a little more on the objective. If the combo was not effective, select a new competency-strength combo that seems likely to help you achieve the objective.

Each time we do this, we improve ourselves in some way. Even the competency-strength experiments that don't work tell us something about ourselves.

Take it easy on yourself but keep trying. Your small wins will keep you going and will point you in the direction of the larger improvements to come.

Keep a record of your efforts and the results in three sections:

1. Combos I will try next (from highest to lowest potential)
2. Combos that worked (from best to barely)
3. Combos that didn't work the first time (from almost to not even close)

Every time you complete a goal, do something to reward yourself. Really. Accomplishing a goal in life is a big deal and should be recognized. Go home early to shop and prepare a special dinner, buy a special bottle of wine, try a new restaurant, see some live entertainment, have a long massage, or sit on the patio and smoke an expensive cigar. Then cycle back to step three and add a new potential goal to replace the one you just accomplished.

When you have achieved two of the goals from your intermediate vision, consider refreshing the vision and creating new goals.

When you have revised the working version of your vision a couple times, revisit your long-range vision. It, too, may need some updating.

Worried that you'll peak someday? Don't be. Working toward your long-range vision is like climbing a mountain with *no* peak. As you periodically redefine it, it will keep rising.

INTENTION AND COMMITMENT

To achieve your goals and move closer to your desired vision of yourself, you have the Level Up Method to create your competency-strength combos, the 7 Step program to set and work on your goals, and two ingredients you will supply—your intention and your commitment.

Intention is what one intends to do.

Intention is what brought you to this book. You know that intention is what gets every successful effort going. Intention got you to the base of the 7 Steps, and intention will drive your early wins.

Commitment is the act of binding oneself to a course of action.

Commitment will keep you dedicated to achieving your goals. Commitment will keep you in the game, motivating you until you produce the results you desire.

INTENTION→7 STEPS→COMMITMENT

Intention. Commitment. They are the forces you will use to get started on your self-development plan and to see the process through to become the next better version of you.

NEED A PARTNER?

If you like having others support you with your projects, consider taking on accountability partners to join you on specific goals or different segments of the 7 Steps. If you ask friends or coworkers to be your partners, offer to help them in some way. Because they are volunteering their time, it is unlikely that one person will be able to dedicate themselves to your entire process. One approach is to consider what kind of support you will need during different stages or with your goals. You may ask a few individuals to help you with specific parts of your plan.

If you wish to have one dedicated partner throughout and have a mentor, lucky you! Mentors, with their combination of wisdom and interest in you, can make wonderful guides and accountability partners. Or, consider engaging a coach. A coach can help bring out your best, will help you create a program tailored just for you, and will help you remain committed to going the distance on your journey of self-development.

> *Everyone needs a coach.*
> *We all need people who give us feedback. That's how we improve.*
> —Bill Gates[93]

High performers in every walk of life have coaches. Athletes, actors, and executives were the first to discover that having a coach helped them post the best performances they were capable of. Now, anyone who wishes to improve some aspect of his life can have his own coach. There are coaches for every purpose: life coaches; health and wellness coaches; relationship coaches; career coaches; executive and leadership coaches; and strengths coaches, who serve high achievers in all sectors.

Like taking a series of different buses to get across town, friends or coworkers can be your partners on different stages of your journey. But if you want to board the express and make a more direct trip with just one partner, engage a mentor or a coach.

---

93 Bill Gates, "Teachers Need Real Feedback," TED Talk, May 2013.

YOUR LEVEL UP DASHBOARD

To keep track of the major ingredients of your plan, we have a template for you—Your Level Up Dashboard. You can find it in Appendix C. Attached to it is Your Continuous Improvement Journal from Chapter 11.

If you keep this somewhere that calls your attention to it, it will help you keep your vision, goals, and competency-strength combos top of mind. You know this is a good idea, right?

CHAPTER 14

Toward the Next Version of You

TIME TO CELEBRATE!

Congratulations are in order. You stuck with this, learning how to use your unique strengths as levers to elevate your competencies and reach your goals. Take a moment to revisit the Table of Contents as a reminder of how far you've come. There is now a lot more of *you*—to think strategically, to navigate change, to build collaborative relationships, to lead people, to drive results, and to live a fulfilling life as you become the next and better version of you. You know how to use the Level Up Method to create your own powerful competency-strength combos. Working the 7 Steps in your way will produce a nice ROI on your investment in yourself. Well done!

And you have advanced through the BIG IDEAS of the Level Up System.

The Big Ideas of Level Up
All in One Place

The BIG IDEA of Part I: Your Strengths is:

The desirable aspects of your character and the unique ways you solve problems and work with others are your strengths. Your most potent ones are called your signature strengths.

Your
CHARACTER TRAITS

+

your
ABILITY TO COMPLETE WORK

=

your
STRENGTHS

The Big Idea of Part II: The Competencies is:

Competencies help us achieve our objectives. We can improve our competencies by intentionally selecting the strengths that will best help us use our competencies to produce the results we desire.

To achieve an
OBJECTIVE

+

select the
COMPETENCY
that will be most effective

+

support it with the
STRENGTH
that will most increase the competency's power.

+

Use this
COMPETENCY-STRENGTH COMBINATION
to

+

produce
RESULTS

The Big Idea of Part III: Your Goals is:

Use your vision, your values, and your strengths to determine the best goals for you.

Your
VISION
for Yourself in the Future

+

Your
VALUES

+

Your signature
STRENGTHS

=

Your
GOALS
for Yourself in the Present

The Big Idea of 7 Steps to Level Up is:

Choose goals that embrace your vision, values, and strengths. Practice using your competency-strength combinations to accomplish these goals and you *will* Level Up.

Your
VISION,
VALUES & STRENGTHS

+

GOALS & OBJECTIVES

+

COMPETENCY-STRENGTH COMBOS
The Level Up Method

+

PRACTICE

=

LEVEL UP!
The Next Better Version of You

You've heard, life is a journey not a destination? Try to get a little better in some way every week. Experience the delight of approaching new issues in new ways, and old issues in new ways:

To learn something new, take the path that you took yesterday.
—John Burroughs

Your strengths and competencies will help you do so. With your powerful competency-strength combinations, you will become more *abundant*. You will have more of what you need to take you where you want to go.

I hope *Level Up* has given you some new energy and an optimism with which to continue *your* expedition toward your vision.

Bon voyage!

APPENDIX A

The 5 Sets of Strengths
and
The 5 Categories of Competencies

THE 5 SETS OF STRENGTHS
AND LOCATIONS OF OUR ENTRIES ON INDIVIDUAL STRENGTHS

1   Thinking Thoroughly: *Increase Wisdom and Make Plans*

with Character Strengths–from VIA

Creativity®	Love of Learning®
Curiosity®	Perspective®
Judgement®	

with Work Strengths–from Gallup

Analytical®	Input®
Context®	Intellection®
Futuristic®	Learner®
Ideation®	Strategic®

2   Interacting with Others: Connect with People and Support Them

with Character Strengths–from VIA

Fairness®	Social Intelligence®
Honesty®	Teamwork®
Love®	

with Work Strengths—from Gallup

Empathy®   Individualization®
Harmony®   Positivity®
Includer®   Relator®

3   Having a Positive Effect on Others: *Respect People and Influence Them*

with Character Strengths—from VIA

Forgiveness®   Kindness®
Humility®   Leadership®
Humor®

with Work Strengths—from Gallup

Communication®   Significance®
Developer®   Woo®
Self-Assurance®

4   Performing with Excellence: *Initiate Action and Carry Out Plans*

with Character Strengths—from VIA

Bravery®   Self-Regulation®
Perseverance®   Zest®
Prudence®

with Work Strengths–from Gallup

Achiever®	Deliberative®
Activator®	Discipline®
Adaptability®	Focus®
Arranger®	Maximizer®
Command®	Responsibility®
Competition®	Restorative®
Consistency®	

5   Aligning to Your Values: *Practice Self-Awareness and Self-Care*

with Character Strengths–from VIA

Appreciation of Beauty and Excellence®

Gratitude®	Spirituality®
Hope®	

with Work Strengths–from Gallup

Belief®	Connectedness®

THE 5 CATEGORIES OF COMPETENCIES
AND THE 17 INDIVIDUAL COMPETENCIES

1   Thinking Strategically
        Creating Vision
        Making Decisions
        Developing Plans

2   Navigating Change
        above, and...
        Tolerating Risk
        Negotiating
        Communicating Clearly

3   Leading People
        above, and...
        Building Collaborative Relationships
        Inspiring Others
        Developing Others
        Influencing Others
        Leading Teams
        Managing Conflict

4   Driving Results
        above, and...
        Taking Initiative
        Executing Efficiently

5   Developing Self
        Continually Learning
        Acting Professionally
        Continuously Improving

APPENDIX B

The Level Up Large List of Values

Find Yours Here

400 examples to help you identify *your* top 3 to 5 core values

Ability
Abundance
Acceptance
Accessibility
Accomplishment
Accuracy
Achievement
Acknowledgement
Activeness
Adaptability
Adoration
Adroitness
Adventure
Affection
Affluence
Aggressiveness
Agility
Alertness
Aliveness
Altruism
Ambition
Amusement

Anticipation
Appreciation
Approachability
Artfulness
Articulacy
Assertiveness
Assurance
Attentiveness
Attractiveness
Audacity
Availability
Awareness
Awe
Balance
Beauty
Beingness
Being the best
Belonging
Benevolence
Bliss
Boldness
Bravery

Brilliance
Briskness
Buoyancy
Calmness
Camaraderie
Candor
Capability
Care
Carefulness
Celebrity
Certainty
Challenge
Charity
Charm
Chastity
Cheerfulness
Clarity
Classiness
Cleanliness
Clear-mindedness
Cleverness
Closeness

Cognizance	Cunningness	Eagerness
Collaboration	Curiosity	Economy
Comfort	Daring	Ecstasy
Commitment	Decisiveness	Education
Compassion	Decorum	Effectiveness
Competence	Deepness	Efficiency
Completion	Deference	Elation
Composure	Delicacy	Elegance
Concentration	Delight	Empathy
Confidence	Dependability	Encouragement
Conformity	Depth	Endurance
Congruency	Desire	Energy
Connection	Determination	Enjoyment
Consciousness	Devotion	Enlightenment
Consistency	Devoutness	Entertainment
Contentment	Dexterity	Enthusiasm
Continuity	Dignity	Exactness
Contribution	Diligence	Excellence
Control	Diplomacy	Excitement
Conviction	Direction	Exhilaration
Conviviality	Directness	Expectancy
Coolness	Discipline	Expediency
Cooperation	Discovery	Experience
Cordiality	Discretion	Expertise
Correctness	Diversity	Exploration
Courage	Dominance	Expressiveness
Courtesy	Dreaming	Extravagance
Craftiness	Drive	Extroversion
Creativity	Duty	Exuberance
Credibility	Dynamism	Facilitating

Fairness
Faith
Fame
Family
Fascination
Fashion
Fearlessness
Ferocity
Fidelity
Fierceness
Financial indepen-
dence
Fineness
Finesse
Firmness
Fitness
Flexibility
Fluency
Fluidity
Focus
Fortitude
Frankness
Freedom
Friendliness
Frugality
Fun
Gallantry
Generosity
Gentility
Giving

Grace
Gratitude
Gregariousness
Growth
Guidance
Happiness
Harmony
Health
Heart
Helpfulness
Heroism
Holiness
Honesty
Honor
Hopefulness
Hospitality
Humility
Humor
Hygiene
Imagination
Impact
Impartiality
Impeccability
Independence
Industry
Ingenuity
Inquisitiveness
Insightfulness
Inspiration
Integrity

Intelligence
Intensity
Intimacy
Intrepidness
Introversion
Intuition
Intuitiveness
Inventiveness
Investing
Joy
Judiciousness
Justice
Keenness
Kindness
Knowledgeable-
ness
Lavishness
Leadership
Learning
Liberation
Liberty
Liveliness
Logic
Longevity
Love
Loyalty
Majesty
Making a differ-
ence
Mastery

Maturity	Pleasantness	Refinement
Meekness	Pleasure	Reflection
Mellowness	Poise	Relaxation
Meticulousness	Polish	Reliability
Mindfulness	Popularity	Religiousness
Moderation	Potency	Resilience
Modesty	Power	Resolution
Motivation	Practicality	Resolve
Mysteriousness	Pragmatism	Resourcefulness
Neatness	Precision	Respect
Nerve	Preeminence	Rest
Obedience	Preparedness	Restraint
Open-mindedness	Presence	Reverence
Openness	Privacy	Richness
Optimism	Proactivity	Rigor
Order	Proficiency	Sacredness
Organization	Professionalism	Sacrifice
Originality	Prosperity	Sagacity
Outlandishness	Prudence	Saintliness
Outrageousness	Punctuality	Sanguinity
Passion	Purity	Satisfaction
Peacefulness	Qualification	Security
Perceptiveness	Quietness	Self-control
Perfection	Quickness	Selflessness
Perseverance	Realism	Self-reliance
Persistence	Readiness	Sensitivity
Persuasiveness	Reason	Sensuality
Philanthropy	Reasonableness	Serenity
Piety	Recognition	Service
Playfulness	Recreation	Sexuality

Sharing
Shrewdness
Significance
Silence
Simplicity
Sincerity
Skillfulness
Smartness
Solidarity
Solidity
Solitude
Soundness
Speed
Spirit
Spirituality
Spontaneity
Stability
Stillness
Strength
Structure
Substantiality
Success
Support
Supremacy
Surprise
Sympathy
Synergy
Tactfulness
Teamwork
Temperance

Thankfulness
Thoroughness
Thoughtfulness
Thrift
Tidiness
Timeliness
Traditionalism
Tranquility
Transcendence
Trust
Trustworthiness
Truth
Understanding
Unflappability
Uniqueness
Unity
Usefulness
Utility
Valor
Variety
Victory
Vigor
Virtue
Vision
Vitality
Vivacity
Warmth
Watchfulness
Wealth
Willfulness

Willingness
Winning
Wisdom
Wittiness
Wonder
Youthfulness
Zeal

APPENDIX C

Your Level Up Dashboard
and
Continuous Improvement Journal

I - My dominant strengths

Strength Thinking   Influencing

1.   1.

2.   2.

3.   3.

Relationship Building   Executing

1.   1.

2.   2.

3.   3.

II - My vision for the next version of me (in 1 to 3 years)

III - My core values

1.

2.

3.

Your Level Up Dashboard *(con'd)*

IV - My top 3 SMART goals

1.

2.

3.

V - Objectives and Competency-Strength combos I will try for each

For Goal 1	Competency-Strength Combo	When/With Whom
1.		
2.		
3.		

For Goal 1	Competency-Strength Combo	When/With Whom
1.		
2.		
3.		

For Goal 1	Competency-Strength Combo	When/With Whom
1.		
2.		
3.		

Your Continuous Improvement Journal

2 min   Think about last week's entry. Rate your progress 1-10.

_____

_____

3 min   What will you try to get better at during the coming week?

_____

_____

_____

5 min   One thing you will do more of:

_____

_____

Which competency-strength combo will you try?

_____

_____

5 min   One thing you will do less of:

_____

_____

Which competency-strength combo will you try?

_____

_____

APPENDIX D

Your Level Up Toolbox

Everything You Need

Life is 10% what happens to you and 90% how you react to it.
—Charles R. Swindoll

Picture you, the high achiever, confidently on your way to a jobsite where you will work on an important project. Wherever you go, know that you bring the resources you have created and accumulated, your:

- knowledge
- experience
- values
- intuition
- intention
- commitment

You now have two more to add to your list:

- the Level Up Method to create the unique competency-strength combos that will help you accomplish any goal, and
- the 7 Step Level Up framework as your personal development program

Working together, your formidable resources will help you post superior results and accelerate your journey toward the best possible version of you.

You also have a new toolbox, brimming with the tools you have recently acquired.

Open the lid. Looks different, doesn't it?

In the top tray are:

- your signature character and work strengths
- your Constellation of Competencies. In each of these strongly bonded competency-strength combos, you have woven a competency and a strength together.

In the second tray are more tools, ones you use less often:

- your intermediate character and work strengths
- all the other competencies

When a job demands, you can move some of these to the top tray, to lend a hand to the strengths and competencies already there, or to form new competency-strength combos to help you accomplish new goals and objectives.

In the big section at the bottom of your toolbox, there for you when you need them, is a large assortment of tools to help you understand and address issues with the competency-strength combinations that will be most effective. While a few of these are classics, most have been created here just for you:

- Strength-Competency-Achievement Model:
  How We and Others Perceive Our Value
- 5 Step Decision-Making Process
- Eisenhower Matrix decision-making model
- Causes, Types, Stages, and Characteristics of Change
- 3 Ways to Improve Your Ability to Tolerate Risk
- 4 Stages of Negotiating
- 5 Elements of Effective Communication
- 4 Stages of Change
- 5 Stages of Communicating Change
- 10 Things Great Team Leaders Do
- 7 Ingredients of Great Teams
- 5 Steps to Manage Conflict
- 5 Key Elements of Executing Efficiently
- 7+ Benefits of Continually Learning
- 7 Ingredients of Acting Professionally
- How to Practice Time Leadership
- 5 Tips on Goal Setting
- 7 Steps to Level Up
- Layered Approach to Goal Setting
- The Scientific Method
- Intentional Change Theory
- Level Up Large List of Values
- Your Continuous Improvement Journal
- Your Level Up Dashboard

How do you like your new toolbox? Are you ready to tackle your plans and be creative with your tools?

Great. Now go out and improve something, or break it so you can fix it to be better than before!

ACKNOWLEDGEMENTS

The wisdom and perceptions of many insightful people can be found here. I am grateful for the fine work they have done, for the interchanges we have had, and for their generous spirits. Two of especially generous spirit are Marshall Goldsmith and Dorie Clark.

Special thanks to Seth Godin, cited here several times. Reading Seth's keen observations often feels like having Will Rogers and Mark Twain in our time. Encouraging us to do more and be more, he is a comforting beacon in the foggy night of our information- and opinion-rich world. It was one of Seth's expressions, level up, and how he uses it that inspired the name of this book. Thanks, Seth!

This book would not be but for Morgan Gist MacDonald and her team at Paper Raven Books. Morgan supported and gently-but-intently guided me every step of the way. She was my superb writing coach, developmental editor, brainstorming partner, publishing team leader, and invaluable accountability partner through the entire process. I found each of her team members at Paper Raven who worked with me on this book to be encouraging collaborators and professional contributors. Thank you, Morgan and Paper Raven!

A heartfelt thank you to my amazing wife, Susan. If I had two virtual tennis partners in creating this book, they were Morgan and Susan. Morgan returned every shot, and launched some of her own, usually just far enough away from me to be a challenge, but not so distant that I had no chance of returning them.

Susan, bless her, played an entirely different game. Sometimes she responded to my driving serve with a gentle lob. Other times, she put a halt to our net volley with a high shot over my head. And sometimes she just let my ball go by, not dignifying it with a response. Her patience, wisdom, love, support—and patience, again—kept me in the game.

I am deeply grateful for the conversations, perspectives, and encouragement of Ben Wigert, Director of Research and Strategy at Gallup. Ben has a profound understanding of the science underlying the study of both competencies and strengths. And he is one of the most energizing conversationalists I have had the pleasure of knowing.

My gratitude to Neal Mayerson and the Mayerson Family Foundations for founding and funding the study of character strengths at the VIA Institute. VIA offers their character strengths assessments and reports to all free of charge.

Thanks to two of the most informative and prolific communicators on work strengths, Jim Collison and Maika Leibbrandt at Gallup. Their insights and perspectives greatly helped me understand how we can use our work strengths to improve our competencies.

I also would like to express my appreciation to each of my Launch Team members for the inspiration each of them has been in my life and the insights and encouragements each has offered along the way of writing this book. Thank you so much, Annie Bennett, Bob Oster, Ward Fredericks, and wife Susan.

DOWNLOADABLE RESOURCES

Thank you for reading *Level Up*. Because you've come this far, you deserve a reward!

To obtain your own working copies of several of the graphics and forms in this book, open

www.readlevelup.com

to unlock the PDFs of your materials.

These are for you to use and share as you wish. The more of us who Level Up, the better!

HELP WITH YOUR JOURNEY...

I hope you have found this exploration of how to become the best possible version of you to be interesting and useful, and that it encourages you to take the next steps in your life.

If you would like some help getting traction on important issues in your life, you may wish to work directly with me at Level Up Advisors.

If we do so, it will be my job and my pleasure to encourage and facilitate your growth in a way that is natural and highly effective for you, as you use your values and strengths to improve and engage the competencies that will enable you to reach your goals.

As your coach and advisor, I will provide the process and a safe and supportive environment—a "crosswalk"—where we can examine your options as you transit from the person you are to the person you desire to be.

To learn how you can Level Up, or to contact me directly, please visit:

www.levelupadvisors.solutions

Earlier in the book, I offered to share my personal strengths and values with you.

Here they are, for no reason other than they might be of some interest or may encourage you to write out your own and appreciate how unique *you* are.

My signature character strengths:

Humor | Appreciation of Beauty and Excellence | Kindness | Hope | Curiosity | Love of Learning

My signature work strengths:

Strategic | Futuristic | Learner | Maximizer | Arranger | Individualization | Achiever | Positivity

My values:

Beauty | Truth | Wisdom, and Humility...

...at how there are endless opportunities to see Beauty, Truth, and Wisdom

All the best to you on your journey. It would be my honor to join you.

INDEX